MEDITATIONS AND READINGS FOR LENT

A version of Christianity
motivated by fear that
sees itself as the victim
of constant attack doesn't
do credit to the beauty +
strength of the Gospel, or
to God Himself, who is present in all things.

MEDITATIONS
and
READINGS
for
LENT

from St. Thomas Aquinas

THOMAS AQUINAS

SCOTTS VALLEY
CALIFORNIA
2010

NIHIL OBSTAT
Ernestus Messenger, Ph.D.
Censor Deputatus

IMPRIMATUR
Joseph Butt, Vic. Gen.
Westmonasterii, die VIIIa Februarii MCMXXXVII

Contents

Septuagesima Sunday

The Work of the Vineyard

Going out about the third hour, he saw others standing in the market-place idle. And he said to them: Go you also into my vineyard, and I will give you what shall be just.—Matt. 20:3.

In these words we may notice four things:

1. The goodness of the Lord, "going out"—that is, for his people's salvation. For that Christ should go out to lead men into the vineyard of justice was indeed an act of infinite goodness.

Our Lord is five times said to have gone out. He went out in the beginning of the world, as a sower, to sow his creatures: "The sower went out to sow his seed." Then in his nativity to enlighten the world: "Until her just one come forth as brightness" (Isa. 62:1). In his Passion to save his own from the power of the devil and from all evil: "My just one is near at hand, my savior is gone forth" (Isa. 51:5). He goes out like the father of a family, caring for his children and his goods: "The kingdom of heaven is like to an householder, who went out early in the morning to hire laborers into his vineyard" (Matt. 20:1). Finally he goes out to judgment, to make most strict inquiry after the wicked, like some overseer, to beat down rebels, like some mighty fighter, and, like a judge, to punish as they merit, criminals and malefactors.

2. The foolishness of men. For nothing is more foolish than that in this present life, where men ought so to work that they may live eternally, men should live in idleness. "He found them in the market place idle." That market-place is this our present life. For it is in the market-place[1] that men quarrel and buy and sell, and so the market-place stands for our life of everyday, full of affairs, of buying and selling, and in which also the prospects of grace and heavenly glory are sold in exchange for good works.

These laborers were called idle because they had already let slip a part of their life. And not evil-doers alone are called idle, but also those who do not do good. And as the idle never attain their end, so will it be with these. The end of man is life eternal. He therefore who works in the proper way will possess that life if he is not an idler.

It is great folly to live in idleness in this life because from idleness, as from an evil teacher, we learn evil knowledge; because through idleness we come to lose the good that lasts forever; because through the short idleness of this life we incur a labor that is eternal.

3. The necessity of working in the vineyard of the Lord. "Go you also into my vineyard."

The vineyard into which the men are sent to work is the life of goodness, in which there are as many trees as there are virtues. We are to work in this vineyard in five ways: Planting in it good works and virtues; rooting up and destroying the thorns—that is, our vices; cutting down the superfluous branches, "Every branch in me, that beareth fruit, he will purge it, that it may bring forth more fruit" (John 15:2); keeping off the little foxes—that is, the devils; and guarding it from the thieves, that is, keeping ourselves indifferent to the praise and the blame of mankind.

4. The usefulness of labor. The wage of those who labor in the

---

1. *Forum* in the Latin text.

vineyard is a penny that out-values thousands of silver crowns. And this is what we are told in Holy Scripture: "The peaceable had a vineyard, every man bringeth for the fruit thereof a thousand pieces of silver (Cant. 8:11). The thousand crowns are the thousand joys of eternity, and these are signified by the penny.

(Sermon for Septuagesima Sunday.)

Monday after Septuagesima

ON DOING GOOD

In doing good let us not fail.
For in due time we shall reap, not failing.—Gal. 11:9.

In these words St. Paul does three things:

1. He warns us that we must do good. For to do good is a duty, seeing that all things, by their nature, teach us to do good.

(i) They so teach us because they are themselves good. "And God saw all the things that he had made, and they were very good" (Gen. 1:31). Sinners have ample cause to make them blush in the multitude of created things all of them good, while sinners themselves are evil.

(ii) Because all things, by their nature, do good. For every creature gives itself, and this is a sign of their own goodness and of the goodness of their Creator. Denis says, "God is goodness, something which must diffuse itself." St. Augustine says, "It is a great sign of the divine goodness, that every creature is compelled to give itself."

(iii) Because all things by their nature desire what is good and tend to the good. The good is, in fact, that for which everything longs.

2. St. Paul warns us that in doing good, we fail not. There are three things which most of all cause a man to persevere in doing good:

(i) Assiduous and wholehearted prayer for help from God lest we yield when we are tempted: "Watch ye, and pray that ye enter not into temptation" (Matt. 26:41).

(ii) Unceasing fearfulness. As soon as a man feels confident he is safe, he begins to fail in doing good: "Unless thou hold thyself diligently in the fear of the Lord, thy house shall quickly be overthrown" (Ecclus. 27:4). Fear of the Lord is the guardian of Life; without it speedily indeed and suddenly is the house thrown down, that is to say, a dwelling place that is of this world.

(iii) Avoidance of venial sins, for venial sins are the occasion of mortal sin and often undermine the achievement of good works. St. Augustine says, "Thou hast avoided dangers that are great; beware lest thou fall victim to the sand."

3. St. Paul offers a reward that is fitting, is generous, and is everlasting. "For in due time we shall reap not failing."

Fitting: "in due time," that is, at a fitting time, at the day of judgment when each shall receive what he has accomplished. So the farmer receives the fruit of his sowing, not immediately but in due time. "The husbandman waiteth for the precious fruit of the earth; patiently bearing till he receive the early and the latter rain" (James 5:7).

Generous: "We shall reap"—here it is the copiousness of the reward that is indicated. With the harvest and reaping we associate abundance: "He who soweth in blessings, shall also reap blessings" (2 Cor. 9:6). "Your reward is very great in heaven" (Matt. 5:12).

(Sermon for the 15th Sunday after Pentecost).

Everlasting: "We shall reap, not failing." We ought then to do good not for an hour merely, but always and continually. In doing good let us not fail—that is to say, let us not fail in working, for we shall not fail in reaping. "Whatsoever thy hand is able to do, do it earnestly" (Eccles. 9:10). And right it is not to fail in working, for the reward to which we are looking is everlasting and unfailing. Whence St. Augustine says: "If man will set no limit to his labor, God will set no limit to the reward."

(In Galatians 6:9.)

Tuesday after Septuagesima

THE PRAYER OF OUR LORD IN THE GARDEN

1. And going a little further, He fell upon his face, praying, and saying: My Father"—Matt. 26:39.

Our Lord here recommends to us three conditions to be observed when we pray.

(i) Solitude: because "going a little further" he separated himself even from those whom he had chosen. "When thou shalt pray, enter into thy chamber, and having shut the door pray to thy Father in secret" (Matt. 6:6). But notice he went not far away but "a little," that He might show that he is not far from those who call upon Him, and also that they might see him praying and learn to pray in like fashion.

(ii) Humility: "He fell upon his face," giving thereby an example of humility. This because humility is necessary for prayer, and because Peter had said: "Yea, though I should die with thee, I will not deny thee" (Matt. 26:35). Therefore did Our Lord fall, to show us we should not trust in our own strength.

(iii) Devotion, when He said, "My Father." It is essential that when we pray we pray from devotion. He says, "My Father," because He is uniquely God's Son; we are God's children by adoption only.

(In Matt. 26.)

2. If it be possible let this chalice pass from me.
Nevertheless not as I will but as Thou wilt—Matt. 26: 39.

Here we consider the tenor of prayer. Christ was praying according to the prompting of his sense nature, in so far, that is, as his prayer, as advocate for his senses, was expressing the inclinations of his senses, proposing to God, by prayer, what the desire of his senses suggested. And He did this that He might teach us three things:

(i) That he had taken a true human nature with all its natural inclinations.

(ii) That it is lawful for man to will, according to his natural inclination, a thing which God does not will.

(iii) That man ought to subject his own inclination to the divine will. Whence St. Augustine says: "Christ, living as a man, showed a certain private human willingness when he said, 'Let this chalice pass from me.' This was human willingness, a man's own will and, so to say, his private desire. But Christ, since He wills to be a man of right heart, a man directed to God, adds, 'Nevertheless not as I will, but as thou wilt.'"   *(3.12.11).*[2]

And in this he teaches by example how we should arrange our inclinations so that they do not come into conflict with the divine rule. Whence we learn that there is nothing wrong in our shrinking from what is naturally grievous, so long as we bring our emotion into line with the divine will.

Christ had two wills, one from his Father in so far as he was God and the other in so far as he was man. This human will he submitted in all things to his Father, giving us in this an example to do likewise, "I came down from heaven, not to do my will, but the will of him that sent me" (John 6:38).   *(In Matt. 26.)*

---

2. *Summa Theologiae*, Part 3, Question 12, Article 11, and similarly for similar references.

Wednesday after Septuagesima

GOOD WORKS

If any man build upon this foundation, gold, silver,
precious stones, wood, hay, stubble, every man's work
shall be manifest. 1 Cor. 3:12–13.

1. The works that man relies on in matters spiritual and divine are compared to gold, silver, and precious stones, things substantial, brilliant, and precious, yet they are compared in such a way that gold symbolizes those things by which man tends to God Himself by contemplation and love. "I counsel thee to buy of me gold fire-tried" (Apoc. 3:18)—that is, wisdom with charity. By silver are meant those acts by which man clings to the spiritual realities he must believe, love, and contemplate. Whence in the Gloss, silver is interpreted as referring to love of one's neighbor. By precious stones is to be understood the work of the different virtues with which man's soul is decked.

Those human activities, on the other hand, by means of which man acquires material goods, are compared to stubble or chaff, worthless rubbish, glittering and easily burnt. There are however grades in this rubbish, some things being more stable than others, some things more easily consumed than the rest. Men themselves, for example, are more worthy than other carnal things, and, by succession, humanity escapes destruction. Men are hence compared to wood. Man's flesh however is easily corrupted by sickness and by death, whence it is compared to hay. All things which make for the glory of such a being speedily come to naught, whence they are compared to chaff or stubble.

To build with gold, silver, and precious stones is therefore to build, upon the foundation of faith, something related to the contemplation of the wisdom of divine things, to the love of God, to a following of the saints, to the service of one's neighbor and to the exercise of virtues. To build with wood, hay, and chaff is to build according to plans that are no more than human, for the convenience of the body, and for outward show.

2. That men occupy themselves with purely human things may come about in three ways:

(i) They may place the whole ultimate purpose of their life in the satisfaction of bodily needs. Now to do this is a mortal sin, and therefore in this way a man does not so much build as destroy the foundation, and lay another of a different kind. For the end or ultimate purpose is the foundation in all that relates to desires.

(ii) They may in using purely corporal things have nothing else in view but the glory of God. In this case they are not building with wood, hay, and chaff, but with gold, silver, and precious stones.

(iii) Although they do not place in purely corporal things the ultimate purpose of life, nor because of them will to act against God, they are more influenced by these things than they ought to be. The result is that they are thereby held back somewhat from a care for the things that are God's, and thus they sin venially. And it is this which is really meant by the phrase about building with wood, hay, and chaff, because activities that relate merely to the care of earthly goods have about them something of a venial fault, since they provoke a love of earthly things that is greater than it should be. It is in fact this love which, according to the degree of its tenacity, is compared to wood, to hay and to chaff.

(In 1 Cor. 3.)

Thursday after Septuagesima

THE REWARD

Every man shall receive his own reward,
according to his own labor.—1 Cor. 3:8.

1. This reward is at once common to all men and particular to each.

(i) It is common to all because that which all shall see and all enjoy is the same, that is to say God. "Then shalt thou abound in delights in the almighty" (Job 22:26). "In that day the Lord of hosts shall be a crown of glory, and a garland of joy to the residue of his people" (Isa. 28:5). And therefore St. Matthew says (20:9) that to every laborer in the vineyard there is given one penny.

(ii) The reward is yet special for each individual. One man shall see more clearly than another, and shall enjoy more fully, according to the measure allotted him. Hence the words in St. John (14:2), "In my father's house there are many mansions," for which reason too, it was said, "Everyone shall receive his own reward."

St. Paul shows how the extent of each one's reward will be measured when he says, "according to his own labor." Not that by this is meant an equality as between the amount of labor and the amount of the reward, for as it is said in 2 Cor. 4:17, "That which is at present momentary and light of our tribulation, worketh for us above measure exceedingly an eternal weight of glory." The equality promised is the equality of proportion, an equality such that where there has been greater labor there will be greater reward.

2. The labor can be considered as greater in three ways:

(i) According to the degree of love that inspires it. It is to this indeed that the essence of the reward the vision and enjoyment of God makes a return. St. John (14:21) says, "He that loveth me, shall be loved of my Father: and I will love him, and will manifest myself to him." Whence it follows that he who labors with greater love, even though the labor entailed is less, will receive more of the essential reward.

(ii) According to the kind of work it is. As in human enterprises the greater rewards go to those whose labor is itself of a more noble character (for example, the architect, though he labors less with his body, receives more than the manual worker), so it is in spiritual matters. He who is engaged in a work itself more noble, even though it be that he has labored less with his body, will receive a greater reward at any rate as far as some accidental privilege of glory. Thus there is a special splendor reserved for those who teach, for the virgins, and for the martyrs.

(iii) According to the amount of work done, and this can be understood in two ways. Sometimes it is the actual larger amount of work which merits the larger reward. This is especially true in what concerns remission of punishment; the longer one fasts, for example, or the more distant the place of one's pilgrimage, the greater the remission merited. So too, there is a greater joy from the greater amount of work done.

Sometimes however, the labor is greater from lack of will to do the work, for the things we do willingly are less laborious in the doing. And in such cases the amount of the labor does not increase the reward. Rather does it reduce the reward. As Isaiah says (40:31), "They shall take wings as eagles, they shall run and not be weary, they shall walk and not faint," and in the preceding verse warning us, "Youths shall faint, and labor, and young men shall fall by infirmity."

(In 1 Cor. 3.)

Friday after Septuagesima

The Need for Caution

Wherefore he that thinketh himself to stand,
let him take heed lest he fall.—1 Cor. 10:12.

1. The case of the Jews who, in punishment, were overthrown in the desert (*ibid.* verse 5) is a warning for us. These words of the Scripture contain four things which should attract the wise man's attention, namely, the multitude of those who fell, for it says, "Wherefore"; then the uncertainty of those who still stand, for it adds, "he that thinketh himself to stand"; thirdly, the need for caution, for it adds, "let him take heed"; and finally the ease with which disaster comes, for it says, "lest he fall."

St. Paul says "wherefore" as if to say these men, for all that they have had the advantage of God's gifts, nevertheless, because of their sins, perished, "wherefore," bearing this in mind, he that thinketh himself, by whatever kind of subtle reasoning, to stand, that is, to be in a state of grace and charity, let him take heed, diligently attending to it, lest he fall, whether by sinning himself or by inducing others to sin. "How art thou fallen from heaven, O Lucifer," says Isaiah (14:12), and the Psalmist, "A thousand shall fall at thy side" (Ps. 90:7), and St. Paul himself, in another place, says therefore, "See how you walk, circumspectly" (Eph. 5:15).

2. We must note that the things which drive us to a fall are numerous.

(i) Weakness, lack of strength; as children, the aged and the sick fall in the natural life. As Isaiah says, "They shall fall through infirmity" (Isa. 40:30). This happens to us through lukewarmness in well doing and through too frequent changing.

(ii) We fall under the weight of our sins, as asses fall under a load that is too heavy. "The workers of iniquity have fallen" (Ps. 35:13). And this happens through our neglect to repent.

(iii) Through a multitude of things drawing us, as a tree or a house falls over on the crowd that tugs at it. We fall in this way by the onrush of enemies.

(iv) The slipperiness of the road, and so we fall as travelers fall into the mud. "Take heed lest thou slip with thy tongue and fall" (Ecclus. 28:30). We fall thus through carelessness in guarding our senses.

(v) A variety of traps, and we fall like the bird taken in the nets. "A just man shall fall seven times" (Prov. 24:16). And this happens through the corruption of created things.

(vi) Ignorance of what one ought to do, and we fall easily as do the blind. "If the blind lead the blind, both fall into the pit" (Matt. 15:14). This comes about through our not learning things necessary to us.

(vii) The example of others who fall, as the angels fell by the example of Lucifer. "A just man falling down before the wicked, is as a fountain troubled by the foot, a spring that has suffered defilement" (Prov. 25:26). And this happens when we imitate the wicked.

(viii) The heaviness of the flesh: for the body when corrupted weighs down the soul, as does a stone that hangs at the neck of a swimmer. "A mountain in falling cometh to naught" (Job 14:18).

And this is what comes of pampering the body.

(In 1 Cor. 10.)

Saturday after Septuagesima

ON REFORMING OURSELVES

Be not conformed to this world, but be reformed
in the newness of your mind, that you may prove
what is the good, and the acceptable,
and the perfect will of God.—Romans 12:2.

1. What is forbidden is the forming of oneself after the pattern of the world. "Be not conformed to this world"—that is, to the things which pass away with time. For this present world is a kind of measure of those things which pass away with time. A man forms himself after the pattern of things transitory when, willingly and lovingly, he gives himself to serve them. Those also form themselves after that pattern who imitate the lives of the worldly. "This then I say and testify in the Lord: That henceforward you walk not as also the Gentiles walk in the vanity of their mind" (Eph. 4:17).

2. We are bidden to undertake a reformation of the interior man when it is said, "But be reformed in the newness of your mind." By "mind" is here meant the reason, considered as the faculty by which man makes judgments about what he ought to do. In man, as God first created him, this faculty existed in all the completeness and vigor it could need. Holy Scripture tells us of our first parents that God "filled their hearts with wisdom and showed them both good and evil" (Ecclus. 17:6). But through sin this faculty declined in power and, as it were, grew old, losing its beauty and its brilliance.

The Apostle warns us to form ourselves again, that is, to recover that completeness and distinction of mind that once was ours. This can indeed be regained by the grace of the Holy Ghost, and we should therefore use every endeavor to share in that grace those who lack that grace that they may obtain it, and those who already have gained it faithfully to progress and persevere. "Be renewed in the spirit of your mind," says St. Paul (Eph. 4:23). Or again, in another sense, be renewed in your external actions—that is to say, "in the newness of your mind," i.e., according to the new thing, grace, which you have internally received.

3. The reason for this warning is that "you may prove what is the will of God." We know what befalls a man whose sense of taste suffers in an illness, how he ceases to have a true judgment of flavors and begins to loathe pleasantly tasting things and to crave

for what is loathsome. So it is with the man whose inclinations are corrupted from his conforming himself to the things of this world. He has no longer a true judgment where what is good for him is concerned. It is only the man whose inclinations are healthy and well directed, whose mind is made new again by grace, who can truly judge what is good and what is not. Therefore on this account is it written, "Be not conformed to this world, but be reformed in the newness of your mind that you may prove"—that is, that you may know by experience. As again it says in the psalm, "Taste and see that the Lord is sweet" (Ps. 33:9).

"What is the will of God"—that is, to say the will by which he wills us to be saved. "This is the will of God: your sanctification" (1 Thess. 4:3).

The will of God is good because God wills that we should will to do what is good, and He leads us to this through His commandments. "I will show thee, O man, what is good, and what the Lord requireth of thee" (Micah 6:8).

The will of God is agreeable in as much as to him who is rightly ordered it is a pleasure to do what God wills us to do.

Nor is the will of God merely useful as a means to achieve our destiny; it is a link joining us with our destiny, and in that respect it is perfect.

Such then is the will of God as those experience it who are not formed after the pattern of this world, but are formed over again in the newness of their minds. As to those who remain in the old staleness, fashioned after the world, they judge the will of God not to be a good but a burden and useless.

(In Rom. 12.)

Sexagesima Sunday

THE SEED

The Sower went out to sow his seed.—Luke 8:4.

1. The keenness of the sower. It is Christ who goes forth, and in three ways. He goes from the bosom of the Father, and yet without a change of place; from Jewry to the Gentiles; from the private depths of wisdom to the public life of teaching. It is Christ who sows. Now the seed is the source of fruit. Whence every good action is due to God. What is it that He sows? "His own seed," says the gospel. That seed is the Word of God. And what does it produce? It produces others, like unto Him from whom itself proceeds, for it makes them sons of God.

2. The obstacle in the way of the seed. The obstacle is threefold, because for the growth of the seed three conditions are necessary, namely, it must be remembered, it must take root in love, it must have loving care. The growth is therefore hindered if in place of the first condition there is flightiness of mind, instead of the second there is hardness of heart, and if, in place of the loving care, there is a development of vices.

(i) "Some fell by the wayside." As the way is free for all who care to walk, so does the heart lie open to every chance thought. So it is that when the word of God falls upon a heart that is careless and vain, it falls by the wayside and is doubly imperiled. St. Matthew speaks of one danger only, that "the birds of the air came and ate it up." St. Luke speaks of two, for the seed is trampled into the ground as well as carried off by the birds. So when the careless receive the word of God, it is crushed by their worthless thoughts or their evil company. Whence great joy for the devil if only he can steal away this seed and trample upon it.

(ii) Hardness of heart. This is contrary to charity, for it is in the nature of love to melt things. Hardness means "locked up in itself" or "narrowed within its own limits," and love, since it causes the lover to be moved to what he loves, is a thing that liberates, widens, pours itself out. St. Matthew says therefore, "some fell upon stony ground," and Ezekiel, "I will take away the stony heart out of your flesh, and I will give you a heart of flesh" (Ezek. 36:26). For there are some men whose hearts are so deprived of love of any kind that they are scarcely flesh and blood at all.

There are others who have indeed a natural affection, but it is slight and "has no deepness." To "have deepness" is to have a power of loving deeply. The man may be said to love deeply who loves all things and whatever he loves for the love of God, and who puts the love of God before all else. There is another type of man that does indeed delight in God, but delights more in things. Men of this sort do not pour themselves out, nor have they much deepness of earth.

The gospel continues, "And they spring up immediately," for they who think deeply, think long, but they whose thought is shallow plunge into action at once, and inevitably pass away quickly. So these men hear quickly, but take no root in what they hear, for they "have no deepness" of earth—that is, in the earth of loving charity.

(iii) Destruction of the fruit. The fruit is lost because when "there ariseth tribulation," each man snatches for what he most loves, and the man who loves wealth looks only to his riches. "And when the sun was up they were scorched"—that is, because they lacked strength. "And because they had not root, they withered away," for God was not their root. Others fell among thorns, anxieties, quarrels, and such like things. And the thorns grew up and choked them.

(In Matt. 13.)

Monday after Sexagesima

THE GOODNESS OF GOD

He that spared not even his own Son, but delivered him up
for us all, how hath he not also, with him,
given us all things?—Romans 8:32.

1. Since the Apostle makes mention of many sons when he says (*ibid.* 5:15), "You have received the spirit of adoption of sons," he now separates this Son from all these by saying his own Son, that is to say, not an adoptive son but a son of his own nature, co-eternal with him, that son of whom the Father says, in St. Matthew (3:17), "This is my beloved Son."

The words "he spared not" mean only that God did not exempt Him from the penalty, for there was not in Him any fault to be matter for sparing. God the Father did not withhold from his Son an exemption from the penalty as a way of adding anything to himself. God is perfect. But he so acted, subjecting his Son to the Passion, because this was useful for us.

This is why St. Paul adds, "but delivered him up for us all," meaning that God exposed Christ to the Passion for the expiation of all our sins. He was delivered for our sins, says Isaiah, and the Lord laid on him the iniquity of us all (53:5–6). God the Father delivered him over to death, decreeing him to take flesh and to suffer, inspiring his human will with a burning love by which, eagerly, he would undergo his Passion. "He delivered himself for us," St. Paul says of Our Lord (Eph. 5:2). Judas, too, and the Jews delivered him, but by an activity external to His.

There is something else to notice in the words "He that spared not his own Son." It is as though it said: "Not only has God given other saints over to suffering for the benefit of mankind, but even his own, proper Son."

2. God's own Son, then, being made over for us, all things have

been given us, for St. Paul adds, "How hath he not also with him," that is, in giving Him to us, "given us all things." In other words, all things thereby are turned to our profit. We are given the highest things of all, namely the Divine Persons, for our ultimate joy. We are given reasoning minds in order to live together with them now. We are given the lower things of creation for our use, not only the things which appeal to us but the things which are hostile. "All things are yours," says St. Paul to us, "and you are Christ's and Christ is God's" (1 Cor. 3:22–23). Whence we may see how evidently true are the words of the Psalm (Ps. 33:10), "There is no want to them that fear him."

(In Rom. 8.)

Tuesday after Sexagesima

THE REMEMBRANCE OF OUR LORD'S PASSION

*Think diligently upon him that endured such opposition
from sinners against himself; that you be not wearied,
fainting in your minds.*—Hebrews 12:3.

1. We are advised to "think diligently," that is, to think upon Him over and over again. "In all thy ways," says Holy Scripture, "think upon him" (Prov. 3:6). The reason for which is that no matter what anxiety may befall us, we have a remedy in the cross.

For there we find obedience to God. "He humbled himself, becoming obedient," says St. Paul (Phil. 2:8). Likewise, we find a loving forethought for those akin to him, shown in the care he had, when upon the very cross, for his mother. We find, too, charity for his fellows, for on the cross he prayed for sinners, "Father, forgive them, for they know not what they do" (Luke 23:34). He showed, also, patience in suffering: "I was dumb and was humbled, and kept silence from good things: and my sorrow was renewed" (Ps. 38:3).

Finally he showed, in all things, a perseverance to the end, for he persevered until death itself. "Father, into thy hands I commend my spirit" (Luke 23:46).

So on the cross we find an example of all the virtues. As St. Augustine says, the cross was not only the gallows where Our Lord suffered in patience; it was a pulpit from which he taught mankind.

2. But what is it that we are "to think," over and over again? Three things:

(i) The kind of Passion it was. He endured opposition,[3] that is, suffering from spoken words. For instance they said, "Vah, thou that destroyest the temple of God" (Matt. 27:40). It is said in the Psalms (Ps. 17:44), "Thou wilt deliver me from the contradictions of the people," and it was foretold that Our Lord should be "a sign which shall be contradicted" (Luke 2:34). St. Paul, in the text, says "such opposition," meaning so grievous and so humiliating an opposition. "O all ye that pass by the way, attend, and see if there be any sorrow like unto my sorrow" (Lamentations 1:12).

(ii) From whom He suffered the Passion. It was "from sinners," from those for whom He was suffering. Christ "died once for our sins, the just for the unjust" (1 Pet. 3:18).

(iii) Who it was that suffered. Before the Passion, from the beginning of the world he had suffered in his members, but in the Passion He suffered in his own person. Whence the words "against himself." "Who his own self," says St. Peter (1 Pet. 2:24), "bore our sins in his body upon the tree."

3. To think diligently upon Our Lord's Passion is a very profitable employment, which is why St. Paul adds, "that you be not wearied, fainting in your minds." The Passion of Christ keeps us from fainting. St. Gregory says, "If we recall the Passion of Christ,

3. The word in the Latin text which St. Thomas has before him is *contradictio*.

nothing seems so hard that it cannot be borne with equanimity." You will not then fail, worn out in spirit, in loyalty to the true faith, nor in the prosecution of good works.

St. Paul again gives a reason for our courageous perseverance when he says, in the following verse, "You have not yet resisted unto blood" (Heb. 12: 4). As though he said, "You must not faint at these anxieties your own troubles cause you. You have not yet borne as much as Christ. For He indeed shed his blood for us."

(In Heb. 12.)

Wednesday after Sexagesima

THE NEED TO BE WATCHFUL

Watch ye therefore because you know not what hour
your Lord will come. —Matt. 24:42.

1. Our Lord warns us to be watchful, placing before us our uncertainty as to when we shall die. He says to us, "The day is not certain. Of two that are working one shall be taken and the other left, and no man can be certain which of the two shall be his lot. Therefore you should be careful and watchful. Watch ye therefore."

Then, too, as St. Jerome says, Our Lord left the moment of life's ending uncertain to help us ever to be watchful. For there are three ways in which man may sin: his senses are idle; or he ceases to move; or he sleeps. Hence, "Watch ye," that your senses may be lifted up in contemplation. "I sleep," says Holy Scripture, "but my heart watcheth" (Cant. 5:2). Likewise, "Watch ye," lest you sleep in death. Whoever occupies himself with good works may be said to watch. "Be sober and watch: because your adversary the devil, as a roaring lion, goeth about seeking whom he may devour" (1 Pet. 5:8). Again, "watch," lest you carelessly fall asleep. "How long wilt thou sleep, O sluggard" (Prov. 6:9).

THURSDAY AFTER SEXAGESIMA

2. "Because you know not what hour your Lord will come." St. Augustine says this is written for the Apostles, for those who lived before us, and for ourselves, and it is necessary for all of us because Our Lord comes to all and comes in two ways. He comes at the end of the world to all men generally, and he comes to each man at his own end, that is, at his death. There is thus a double coming, and in each case God has willed that its hour should be uncertain. Moreover these two comings answer each to the other, for the second will find us as we were found at the first. As St. Augustine says, "The World's last day finds unprepared all those whom their own last day found in like condition."

Our Lord's words "Watch ye therefore" and the rest may also be understood with reference to the unseen coming of the Lord into our souls. "If he come to me," it is written in Sacred Scripture, "I shall not see him" (Job 9:11). And so it is that He comes to many and they do not see Him. Therefore should we watch with much carefulness, so that when He knocks we may open to Him. "Behold I stand at the gate and knock. If any man shall hear my voice and open to me the door, I will come in to him, and will sup with him and he with me" (Apoc. 3:20).

(In Matt. 24)

Thursday after Sexagesima

OUR WATCH MUST BE CEASELESS

But this know ye, that if the goodman of the house knew
at what hour the thief would come, he would certainly watch,
and not suffer his house to be broken open.—Matt. 24:43.

Since we are uncertain which hour it will be, we must watch the whole night long.

The house is the soul. Therein man should be at rest. "When

I go into my house," that is, into my conscience, "I shall repose myself with her" (Wisdom 8:16). The goodman of the house is as that "king, that sitteth on the throne of judgment, who scattereth away all evil with his look" (Prov. 20:8).

Sometimes a thief breaks into the house. The thief is any plausible false theory, or indeed any temptation. It is said to be a thief in the sense of the gospel, "He that entereth not by the door into the sheepfold, but climbeth up another way, the same is a thief and a robber" (John 10:1). The door is an excellent name for natural knowledge or natural rights. Whoever enters through his reason, enters through the door. But whoever comes in through desires, or through wrath or the like, is a thief.

Thieves work by night. We have no fear of what comes to us in the day. So it is that temptations never come to the man whose mind is given to contemplation of divine things. Let him however slacken in that service, and presently comes temptation. Hence the timely prayer of Holy Scripture, "When my strength shall fail, do not Thou forsake me" (Ps. 70:9).

We must then watch, since we know not when the Lord shall come, shall come that is, to judgment. Or perhaps we may refer it to the day we shall die. "For yourselves know perfectly, that the day of the Lord shall so come as a thief in the night, for when they shall say peace and security, then shall sudden destruction come upon them" (1 Thess. 5:23). "Wherefore," says Our Lord, "be you also ready, because at what hour you know not the Son of Man shall come" (Matt. 24:44).

St. John Chrysostom notes that men attached to their property will sit up all the night to watch over it. If they can be so watchful for the things that pass away, how much more should they not be watchful over spiritual treasures.

We may notice also a parable of St. Augustine's. There are three servants and they look forward affectionately to the return of their master. The first says, "My lord will come quickly, therefore I shall watch for him." The second says, "My lord will be late, but I will watch none the less." The third says, "At what hour my lord will come I know not, and for this reason I will take care to watch." Which servant spoke best? St. Augustine says the third. The first risks a sad deception, for if he thinks the lord will soon arrive, and in fact the lord is delayed, the servant runs the danger of sleeping through weariness. The second, too, may find he has made a mistake, but he runs no danger. But it is the third who does well, for being uncertain he is continually on the alert. It is therefore a misfortune to fix in our minds any special time.

(In Matt. 24.)

Friday after Sexagesima

THE WORSHIP DUE TO GOD

Thou shalt not have strange Gods before me.—Exod. 20:3.

We are forbidden to worship any but the one God, and there are five things which show the prohibition to be reasonable.

1. God's dignity. If this is disregarded, we insult God. To all dignity is due proper reverence. And we call a man a traitor who refuses to do the King due reverence. This is what some men do with respect to God. "They changed the glory of the incorruptible God into the likeness of the image of a corruptible man, and of birds, and of four-footed beasts, and of creeping things," says St. Paul (Romans 1:23). And this is the most serious of all offenses against God.

2. God's bountifulness. Every good thing we possess comes from God. It is in fact part of God's dignity that he is the maker and giver of all good things. "When thou openest thy hand, all things shall be filled with good" (Ps. 103:28). You are therefore ungrateful beyond measure if you do not recognize that the good you have is his gift.

Nay, you make to yourself another god as truly as the children of Israel, delivered from Egypt, made themselves an idol. This is to be like the harlot of whom the prophet writes, "I will go after my lovers that give me my bread and my water, my wool and my flax, my oil and my drink" (Hosea 2:5).

This sin is also committed by those who place their hope in another than God, that is, when they seek help from another in preference to asking it from God. "Blessed is the man whose trust is in the name of the Lord" (Ps. 39:5), and St. Paul marvels at the Galatians, "But now, after that you have known God, or are rather known by God, how turn you again to the weak and needy elements, which you desire to serve again?" (Gal. 4:9).

3. Our promises. We have renounced the devil and pledged our fidelity to God alone. This pledge we must keep unbroken. "A man making void the law of Moses, dieth without any mercy, under two or three witnesses. How much more do you think he deserveth worse punishment, who hath trodden underfoot the Son of God, and hath esteemed the blood of the testament unclean, by which he was sanctified, and hath offered an affront to the Spirit of Grace?" (Heb. 10:28–29).

"The woman that hath an husband, whilst her husband liveth she shall be called an adulteress, if she be with another man" (Rom. 7:3), and such deserves to be burned. Woe to the sinner, to whoever enters the land by a double way, to those who limp one foot on each side of the division.

4. The weight of the devil's yoke. "You shall serve strange gods day and night," says the Prophet, "which shall not give you any rest" (Jer. 16:13). For the devil does not rest content with one sin, but, the first sin committed, strives all the more to induce us to another. Whoever commits sin is the slave of sin. Hence it is not an easy thing to find one's way out from sin. St. Gregory says, "The sin which is not lightened by penance, soon, by its very weight, drags us to further sin."

SATURDAY AFTER SEXAGESIMA

It is the very contrary that is characteristic of God's dominion over us. For God's commands are not burdensome. "My yoke is sweet and my burden is light" (Matt. 11:30). A man is accounted as doing enough if he does for God as much as he has done for sin. St. Paul, for example, says, "As you have yielded your members to serve uncleanness and iniquity, unto iniquity; so now yield your members to serve justice, unto sanctification" (Rom. 6:19). But of the slaves of the devil the Scripture says, "We wearied ourselves in the way of iniquity and destruction, and have walked through hard ways" (Wis. 5:7), and also, "They have labored to commit iniquity" (Jer. 9:5).

5. The immensity of our reward. No law promises so great a recompense as that which we are promised in the law of Christ. To the Saracens are offered rivers of milk and honey; to the Jews, the promised land; but to Christians, angelic glory. "They shall be as the angels of God in heaven" (Matt. 22:30). Thinking on this St. Peter says, in the Gospel, "Lord to whom shall we go? Thou hast the words of eternal life" (John 6:69).

(In Decalog. 12.)

Saturday after Sexagesima

How Are We to Serve God?

1. We must serve God both by external acts and by internal acts. We are possessed of a double nature; we are intellectual beings and sentient beings also. We should therefore offer to God a double adoration—a spiritual adoration, consisting in the interior devotion of the mind, and a bodily adoration made up of the external humiliation of the body. And since in all acts done in acknowledgment that God is God the external act depends on the internal for the internal act is the more important—so the external acts of

adoration are done for the sake of the internal adoration. That is to say, that it is by our gestures of humility that we are moved to subject ourselves to God in our inclinations and our will. This is due to our nature being what it is, for it is natural to man to proceed to things that can only be known through the intelligence from the starting point of things seen, felt, heard, and known by the senses. So, just as prayer has its origin as something in the mind, and is only in the second place expressed in words, adoration also consists, primarily and in its origin, in an internal reverence of God and only secondarily in certain bodily signs that we are humbling ourselves: such bodily signs, for example, as genuflections to show our weakness by comparison with God, or prostrations to show that we are nothing of ourselves.   *(2-2.84.11.)*

2. In doing external acts we must use a certain measure of discretion. The attitude of a religious man toward the acts by which he acknowledges God to be God is quite different according as those acts are internal or external. It is principally in the internal acts, the acts by which he believes, hopes, and loves, that man's good consists and what makes man good in God's sight. Whence it is written, "The kingdom of God is within you" (Luke 17:21). Man's good and what makes man good in God's sight does not, principally, consist in external acts. "The kingdom of God is not meat and drink," says St. Paul (Rom. 15:17).

Whence the internal acts are as the end, the thing that is to say, which is sought for its own sake: the external acts, through which the body is shown as God's creature, are but as means, i.e., things directed to and existing for the sake of the end.

Now when it is a question of seeking the end, we do not measure our energy or resource, but the greater the end the better our endeavor.

When, on the other hand, it is a question of things we only seek because of the end, we measure our energy according to the relation of the things to the end. Thus a physician restores health as much as he possibly can. He does not give as much medicine as he possibly can, but only just so much as he sees to be necessary for the attainment of health.

In a similar way, man puts no measure to his faith, his hope, and his charity, but the more he believes, hopes, and loves, so much the better man he is. That is why it is said, "Thou shalt love the Lord thy God, with thy whole heart, and with thy whole soul, and with thy whole strength" (Deut. 6:5).

But in the external actions we must use discretion and make charity the measure of our use of them.

(In Rom. 12.)

Quinquagesima Sunday

HOW WE SHOULD SERVE GOD ON THE LORD'S DAY

Remember that thou keep holy the Sabbath Day.—Exod. 20:8.

Man is bound to keep feast days holy. Now a thing is said to be holy in one of two ways—either because the thing is itself unspotted, or because it is consecrated to God. We must say something then of the kind of works from which we should abstain on such days and also of the kind with which we should occupy ourselves.

1. Sacrifices. In Sacred Scripture (Num. 28:3) it is related how God commanded that every day, in the morning and again in the evening, a lamb should be offered up, but that on the sabbath this offering should be doubled. This teaches us that we too ought on the sabbath to offer a sacrifice, a sacrifice taken from all that we possess.

(i) We ought to make an offering of our soul, lamenting our sins and giving thanks for the benefits we have received. "Let my prayer, Lord, be directed as incense in thy sight" (Ps. 140:2). Feast days are instituted to give us spiritual joy, and the means to this is prayer. Whence on such days we should multiply our prayers.

(ii) We should offer our body. "I beseech you therefore brethren, says St. Paul, by the mercy of God, that you offer your bodies a living sacrifice, holy, pleasing unto God" (Rom. 12:1). And we should give praise to God. The psalm says, "The sacrifice of praise shall glorify me" (Ps. 49:23). Wherefore on feast days hymns should be numerous.

(iii) We should offer our goods, and this by giving alms by giving on feast days a double amount, for these are times of universal rejoicing.

2. Study of the word of God. This indeed was the practice of the Jews, as we read in the Acts of the Apostles (13:27). "The voices of the prophets, which are read every sabbath." Christians therefore, whose spiritual state should be more perfect than that of the Jews, ought on such days to meet together for sermons and for the Church's office. And likewise for profitable conversation. Here are two things truly profitable for the soul of the sinner, sure means to his amendment. For the word of God instructs the ignorant and stirs up those that are lukewarm.

3. Direct occupation with the things of God. This do those who are perfect. In the psalms (33:9) we read, "Taste and see that the Lord is sweet," and this because He gives rest to the soul. For just as the body worn out with toil craves for rest, so too does the soul. Now the soul's place is God. "Be thou unto me a God, a protector and a place of refuge," is written in the Psalms (30:3). And St. Paul, too, says, "There remaineth therefore a day of rest for the people of God; for he that is entered into his rest, the same also hath rested from his works, as God did from his" (Heb. 4:9, 10). Again in the book of Wisdom (8:16), "When I go into my house," that is, my conscience, "I shall repose with her," that is, with Wisdom.

But before the soul can attain to this peace, it must already have found peace in three other ways.

It must have peace from the uneasiness of sin. "The heart of the wicked man is like a raging sea, which cannot rest" (Isa. 57:20).

It must have peace from the attractions of bodily desires. "For the flesh lusteth against the spirit, and the spirit against the flesh" (Gal. 5:17).

It must have peace from the cares of everyday life. "Martha, Martha, thou art careful and art troubled about many things" (Luke 10:41).

But after these are attained the soul shall truly rest in God. "If thou call the sabbath delightful, then shalt thou be delighted in the Lord" (Is. 58:14). It is for this that the saints have left all things, for this is that treasure "which a man having found, hid it, and for joy thereof goeth and selleth all that he hath, and buyeth" (Matt. 13:44). For this is the peace of eternal life and of the joy that shall last for ever: "This is my rest forever and ever: here I dwell, for I have chosen it" (Ps. 131:4).

(In Decalog. 17.)

Monday after Quinquagesima

HOLINESS

The gospel says (Luke 1:75), "That we may serve him in holiness and justice." But to serve God is an act of religion. Therefore religion is the same thing as holiness.

The word "holiness" seems to imply two things.

(i) Cleanness, and in this it accords with the Greek word *agios* which means "free of earth." Earth → "dust" / ash

(ii) Firmness, whence, of old, those things were called holy which were protected by the law and thereby rendered inviolable. Whence also things are said to be sanctioned, because they are defended by law. Things which belong to the worship of God may be said to be holy in both of the senses just described. Not only men, therefore, but the temple and the vessels and so forth are said to be made holy from the fact that they are used in the service of God.

Cleanness is essential if the human mind is to be applied to God, because what stains the human mind is its being joined to lower things—as all kinds of things are cheapened by mixture with things less valuable, for example, silver when it is mixed with lead. Now if the mind is to be united to the highest thing of all, i.e., to God, it must be altogether taken away from the things that are lower. And that is why a mind that is lacking in purity cannot be applied to God. "Follow peace with all men and holiness,[4] without which no man shall see God" (Heb. 12:14).

Firmness, too, is required in whoever would set his mind to God. The mind must be set to God as to one's last end and first beginning. But ends and beginnings are the kinds of things which above all others need to be immovable. Whence St. Paul says, "I am sure that neither death nor life, nor angels, nor principalities, nor powers, nor things present nor things to come, nor might, nor height, nor depth, nor any other creatures, shall be able to separate us from the love of God, which is in Christ Jesus, Our Lord" (Romans 13:38–39).

Holiness is then the quality whereby men apply themselves and their actions to God. Hence it does not differ from religion as though it had a different essence, but only according to the way these two things exist. For religion gives God the service due to him in what particularly concerns divine worship in sacrifices, for example, in offerings and in other things of that kind. Holiness, however, gives to God not only these things but the acts of the other virtues too, or again, it ensures that by good works a man makes himself fit for the service of God in worship.

(2-2.81.8.)

---

4.   *Sanctimoniam* in the Latin text which St. Thomas is using.

Tuesday after Quinquagesima

OUR LORD IS SCOURGED

*Having scourged Jesus, he delivered him to them
to be crucified.*—Matt. 27:26.

Why did he scourge him before he delivered him to them? St. Jerome says because it was a Roman custom that prisoners condemned to death should be scourged before execution. So it was that the prophecy was fulfilled, "I was made ready by a scourging" (Ps. 37:18).

Some writers think that Pilate had Our Lord scourged that the Jews might be moved to pity and so, once He was scourged, they would let him go.

Pilate therefore took Jesus and scourged him (John 19:1). He did not, that is, scourge him with his own hands but handed him over to the soldiers. And this that the Jews, sated with his sufferings, might be softened somewhat and cease to rage for his death. For it is the natural thing that a man's anger dies down when he sees the cause of his anger humiliated and punished. This is true of anger, for anger seeks to inflict harm only to a certain degree. But it is not true of hatred, for hatred seeks utterly to destroy the thing hated. Hence the words of Sacred Scripture, "If an enemy findeth an opportunity, he will not be satisfied with blood" (Ecclus. 12:16).

Now it was hatred that moved the Jews against Christ, and therefore it did not satisfy them to see him scourged. "I have been scourged all the day," says the Psalm (72:14), and in Isaiah (50:6) we read, "I have given my body to the strikers."

Did Pilate's intention excuse him from the guilt of scourging Our Lord? By no means, for no action which is bad in itself can be made wholly good by the good intention with which it is done. But to inflict injury on one who is innocent, and especially on the

Son of God, is of all things the one most evil in itself. No intention therefore could possibly excuse it.

(In John 19.)

Ash Wednesday

Death

By one man sin entered into this world,
and by sin death.—Rom. 5:12.

1. If for some wrongdoing a man is deprived of some benefit once given to him, that he should lack that benefit is the punishment of his sin.

Now in man's first creation he was divinely endowed with this advantage that, so long as his mind remained subject to God, the lower powers of his soul were subjected to the reason and the body was subjected to the soul.

But because by sin man's mind moved away from its subjection to God, it followed that the lower parts of his mind ceased to be wholly subjected to the reason. From this there followed such a rebellion of the bodily inclination against the reason, that the body was no longer wholly subject to the soul.

Whence followed death and all the bodily defects. For life and wholeness of body are bound up with this, that the body is wholly subject to the soul, as a thing which can be made perfect is subject to that which makes it perfect. So it comes about that, conversely, there are such things as death, sickness, and every other bodily defect, for such misfortunes are bound up with an incomplete subjection of body to soul.

2. The rational soul is of its nature immortal, and therefore death is not natural to man in so far as man has a soul. It is natural to his body, for the body, since it is formed of things contrary to

each other in nature, is necessarily liable to corruption, and it is in this respect that death is natural to man.

But God who fashioned man is all powerful.

And hence, by an advantage conferred on the first man, He took away that necessity of dying which was bound up with the matter of which man was made. This advantage was however withdrawn through the sin of our first parents.

Death is then natural, if we consider the matter of which man is made and it is a penalty, inasmuch as it happens through the loss of the privilege whereby man was preserved from dying.

(2-2.164.1.)

3. Sin—original sin and actual sin—is taken away by Christ, that is to say, by Him who is also the remover of all bodily defects. "He shall quicken also your mortal bodies, because of his Spirit that dwelleth in you" (Rom. 8:11).

But, according to the order appointed by a wisdom that is divine, it is at the time which best suits that Christ takes away both the one and the other, i.e., both sin and bodily defects.

Now it is only right that, before we arrive at that glory of impassibility and immortality which began in Christ, and which was acquired for us through Christ, we should be shaped after the pattern of Christ's sufferings. It is then only right that Christ's liability to suffer should remain in us too for a time, as a means of our coming to the impassibility of glory in the way He himself came to it.

(1-2.85.5 ad 2.)

Thursday

FASTING

1. We fast for three reasons.

(i) To check the desires of the flesh. So St. Paul says, "in fastings, in chastity" (2 Cor. 6:5), meaning that fasting is a safeguard for chastity. As St. Jerome says, "Without Ceres and Bacchus, Venus would freeze," as much as to say that lust loses its heat through spareness of food and drink.

(ii) That the mind may more freely raise itself to contemplation of the heights. We read in the book of Daniel that it was after a fast of three weeks that he received the revelation from God (Dan. 10:2–4).

(iii) To make satisfaction for sin. This is the reason given by the prophet Joel: "Be converted to me with all your heart, in fasting and in weeping and in mourning" (Joel 2:12). And here is what St. Augustine writes on the matter: "Fasting purifies the soul. It lifts up the mind, and it brings the body into subjection to the spirit. It makes the heart contrite and humble, scatters the clouds of desire, puts out the flames of lust and the true light of chastity."

2. There is commandment laid on us to fast. For fasting helps to destroy sin, and to raise the mind to thoughts of the spiritual world. Each man is then bound, by the natural law of the matter, to fast just as much as is necessary to help him in these matters. Which is to say that fasting in general is a matter of natural law. To determine, however, when we shall fast and how, according to what suits and is of use to the Catholic body, is a matter of positive law. To state the positive law is the business of the bishops, and what is thus stated by them is called ecclesiastical fasting, in contradistinction with the natural fasting previously mentioned.

3. The times fixed for fasting by the Church are well chosen. Fasting has two objects in view:

(i) the destruction of sin; and

(ii) the lifting of the mind to higher things.

The times self-indicated for fasting are then those in which men are especially bound to free themselves from sin and to raise their minds to God in devotion. Such a time especially is that which precedes that solemnity of Easter in which baptism is administered and sin thereby destroyed, and when the burial of Our Lord is recalled, for "we are buried together with Christ by baptism into death" (Rom. 6:4). Then, too, at Easter most of all, men's minds should be lifted, through devotion to the glory of that eternity which Christ in his resurrection inaugurated.

Wherefore the Church has decreed that immediately before the solemnity of Easter we must fast, and, for a similar reason, that we must fast on the eves of the principal feasts, setting apart those days as opportune to prepare ourselves for the devout celebration of the feasts themselves.

(2-2.97.1, 3, 5.)

Friday

The Crown of Thorns

Go forth, ye daughters of Sion, and see king Solomon
in the diadem, wherewith his mother crowned him in the day
of his espousals, and in the day of the joy of his heart.—Cant. 3:11.

This is the voice of the Church inviting the souls of the faithful to behold the marvelous beauty of her spouse. For the daughters of Sion, who are they but the daughters of Jerusalem, holy souls, the citizens of that city which is above, who with the angels enjoy the peace that knows no end, and, in consequence, look upon the glory of the Lord?

1. "Go forth"—shake off the disturbing commerce of this world

so that, with minds set free, you may be able to contemplate him whom you love. "And see king Solomon," the true peacemaker, that is to say, Christ Our Lord.

"In the diadem wherewith his mother crowned him," as though the Church said, "Look on Christ garbed with flesh for us, the flesh He took from the flesh of his mother." For it is his flesh that is here called a diadem, the flesh which Christ assumed for us, the flesh in which he died and destroyed the reign of death, the flesh in which, rising once again, he brought to us the hope of resurrection.

This is the diadem of which St. Paul speaks: "We see Jesus for the suffering of death crowned with glory and honor" (Heb. 2:9). His mother is spoken of as crowning him because Mary the Virgin it was who from her own flesh gave him flesh.

"In the day of his espousals," that is, in the hour of his Incarnation, when he took to himself the Church "not having spot or wrinkle" (Eph. 5:27), the hour again when God was joined with man. "And in the day of the joy of his heart." For the joy and the gaiety of Christ is for the human race salvation and redemption. And coming home, he calls together his friends and neighbors saying to them, "Rejoice with me, because I have found my sheep that was lost" (Luke 15:6).

2. We can however refer the whole of this text simply and literally to the Passion of Christ. For Solomon, foreseeing through the centuries the Passion of Christ, was uttering a warning for the daughters of Sion, that is, for the Jewish people.

"Go forth and see king Solomon," that is, Christ, in his diadem, that is to say, the crown of thorns with which his mother the Synagogue has crowned him; "in the day of his espousals," the day when he joined to himself the Church; "and in the day of the joy of his heart," the day in which he rejoiced that by his Passion he was delivering the world from the power of the devil. "Go forth," therefore, and leave behind the darkness of unbelief, and "see," understand with your minds, that he who suffers as man is really God.

"Go forth," beyond the gates of your city, that you may see him, on Mount Calvary, crucified.

(In Cant. 3.)

Saturday

The Grain of Wheat

*Unless the grain of wheat falling into the ground die,
itself remaineth alone.*—John 12:24.

We use the grain of wheat in two ways, for bread and for seed. Here the word is to be taken in the second sense, grain of wheat meaning seed, and not the matter out of which we make bread. For in this sense it never increases so as to bear fruit. When it is said that the grain must die, this does not mean that it loses its value as seed, but that it is changed into another kind of thing. So St. Paul (1 Cor. 15:36) says, "That which then thou sowest is not quickened, except it die first."

The Word of God is a seed in the soul of man, in so far as it is a thing introduced into man's soul, by words spoken and heard, in order to produce the fruit of good works: "The seed is the Word of God" (Luke 8:11). So also the Word of God garbed in flesh is a seed placed in the world, a seed from which great crops should grow, whence it is compared in St. Matthew's Gospel (13:31–32) to a grain of mustard seed.

Our Lord therefore says to us, "I came as seed, something meant to bear fruit and therefore I say to you, Unless the grain of wheat falling into the ground die, itself remaineth alone" which is as much as to say, "Unless I die, the fruit of the conversion of the Gentiles will not follow." He compares himself to a grain of wheat because he came to nourish and to sustain the minds of men, and to nourish and sustain are precisely what wheaten bread does for men. In the Psalms it is written, "That bread may strengthen man's heart" (Ps. 103:15), and in St. John, "The bread that I will give is my flesh for the life of the world" (John 6:52).

2. "But if it die it bringeth forth much fruit" (John 12:25). What is here explained is the usefulness of the Passion. It is as though the gospel said: "Unless the grain fall into the earth through the humiliations of the Passion, no useful result will follow, for the grain itself remaineth alone. But if it shall die, done to death and slain by the Jews, it bringeth forth much fruit." For example:

(i) The remission of sin. "This is the whole fruit, that the sin thereby should be taken away" (Isaiah 27:9). And this is the fruit of the Passion of Christ as is declared by St. Peter, "Christ died once for our sins, the just for the unjust that he might offer us to God" (1 Pet. 3:18).

(ii) The conversion of the Gentiles to God. "I have appointed you that you shall go forth and bring forth fruit and that your fruit should remain" (John 15:16). This fruit the Passion of Christ bore: "If I be lifted tip from the earth, I will draw all things to myself" (John 12:32).

(iii) The fruit of Glory. "The fruit of good labors is glorious" (Wis. 3:15). And this fruit also the Passion of Christ brought forth: "We have therefore a confidence in the entering into the Holies by the blood of Christ: a new and living way which he hath dedicated for us through the veil, that is to say, his flesh" (Heb. 10:19).

(In John 12.)

First Week in Lent—Sunday

IT WAS FITTING THAT CHRIST SHOULD BE TEMPTED

Jesus was led by the spirit into the desert,
to be tempted by the devil.—Matt. 4:1.

Christ willed to be tempted:

1. That he might assist us against our own temptations. St. Gregory says, "That our Redeemer, who had come on earth to be killed, should will to be tempted was not unworthy of him. It was indeed but just that he should overcome our temptations by his own, in the same way that he had come to overcome our death by his death."

2. To warn us that no man, however holy he be, should think himself safe and free from temptation. Whence again His choosing to be tempted after His baptism, about which St. Hilary says, "The devil's wiles are especially directed to trap us at times when we have recently been made holy, because the devil desires no victory so much as a victory over the world of grace." Whence, too, the scripture warns us, "Son, when thou comest to the service of God, stand in justice and in fear, and prepare thy soul for temptation" (Ecclus. 2:1).

3. To give us an example how we should over come the temptations of the devil, St. Augustine says: "Christ gave himself to the devil to be tempted, that in the matter of our overcoming those same temptations He might be of service not only by his help but by his example too."

4. To fill and saturate our minds with confidence in His mercy. "For we have not a high-priest who cannot have compassion on our infirmities, but one tempted in all things, like as we are, without sin" (Heb. 4:15).

(3.41.1.)

First Monday

CHRIST HAD TO BE TEMPTED IN THE DESERT

He was in the desert forty days and forty nights:
and was tempted by Satan.—Mark 1:13.

1. It was by Christ's own will that he was exposed to the temptation by the devil, as it was also by his own will that he was exposed to be slain by the limbs of the devil. Had He not so willed, the devil would never have dared to approach him.

The devil is always more disposed to attack those who are alone, because, as is said in Sacred Scripture, "If a man shall prevail against one, two shall with stand him easily" (Eccles. 4:12). That is why Christ went out into the desert, as one going out to a battle-ground, that there he might be tempted by the devil. Whereupon St. Ambrose says that Christ went into the desert for the express purpose of provoking the devil. For unless the devil had fought, Christ would never have overcome him for me.

St. Ambrose gives other reasons, too. He says that Christ chose the desert as the place to be tempted for a hidden reason, namely that he might free from his exile Adam who, from Paradise, was driven into the desert; and again that he did it for a reason in which there is no mystery, namely, to show us that the devil envies those who are tending toward a better life.

2. We say with St. Chrysostom that Christ exposed himself to the temptation because the devil most of all tempts those whom he sees alone. So in the very beginning of things he tempted the woman, when he found her away from her husband. It does not however follow from this that a man ought to throw himself into any occasion of temptation that presents itself.

Occasions of temptation are of two kinds. One kind arises from man's own action, when, for example, man himself goes near to sin, not avoiding the occasion of sin. That such occasions are to be avoided we know, and Holy Scripture reminds us of it. "Stay not in any part of the country round about Sodom" (Gen. 19:17). The second kind of occasion arises from the devil's constant envy of those who are tending to better things, as St. Ambrose says, and this occasion of temptation is not one we must avoid. So, according to St. John Chrysostom, not only Christ was led into the desert by the Holy Ghost, but all the children of God who possess the Holy Ghost are led in like manner. For God's children are never content to sit down with idle hands, but the Holy Ghost ever urges them to undertake for God some great work. And this, as far as the devil is concerned, is to go into the desert, for in the desert there is none of that wickedness which is the devil's delight. Every good work is as it were a desert to the eye of the world and of our flesh, for good works are contrary to the desire of the world and of our flesh.

To give the devil such an opportunity of temptation as this is not dangerous, for it is much more the inspiration of the Holy Ghost, who is the promoter of every perfect work, that prompts us than the working of the devil who hates them all.

(3.41.2.)

First Tuesday

CHRIST UNDERWENT EVERY KIND OF SUFFERING

"Every kind of suffering." The things men suffer may be understood in two ways. By "kind" we may mean a particular, individual suffering, and in this sense there was no reason why Christ should suffer every kind of suffering, for many kinds of suffering are contrary the one to the other, as for example, to be burnt and to be drowned. We are of course speaking of Our Lord as suffering from causes outside himself, for to suffer the suffering effected by internal causes, such as bodily sickness, would not have become him. But if by "kind "we mean the class, then Our Lord did suffer by every kind of suffering, as we can show in three ways:

1. By considering the men through whom he suffered. For he suffered something at the hands of Gentiles and of Jews, of men and even of women as the story of the servant girl who accused St. Peter goes to show. He suffered, again, at the hands of rulers, of their ministers, and of the people, as was prophesied: "Why have the Gentiles raged; and the people devised vain things? The kings of the earth stood up, and the princes met together against the Lord and against his Christ" (Ps. 2:1–2).

He suffered, too, from his friends, the men he knew best, for Peter denied him and Judas betrayed him.

2. If we consider the things through which suffering is possible. Christ suffered in the friends who deserted him, and in his good name through the blasphemies uttered against him. He suffered in the respect, in the glory, due to him through the derision and contempt bestowed upon him.

He suffered in things, for he was stripped even of his clothing; in his soul, through sadness, through weariness and through fear; in his body through wounds and the scourging.

3. If we consider what he underwent in his various parts. His head suffered through the crown of piercing thorns, his hands and feet through the nails driven through them, his face from the blows and the defiling spittle, and his whole body through the scourging.

He suffered in every sense of his body. Touch was afflicted by the scourging and the nailing, taste by the vinegar and gall, smell by the stench of corpses as he hung on the cross in that place of the dead which is called Calvary. His hearing was torn with the voices of mockers and blasphemers, and he saw the tears of his mother and of the disciple whom he loved. If we only consider the amount of suffering required, it is true that one suffering alone, the least indeed of all, would have sufficed to redeem the human race from all its sins. But if we look at the fitness of the matter, it had to be that Christ should suffer in all the kinds of sufferings.

(3.46.5.)

First Wednesday

How Great Was the Sorrow of Our Lord in His Passion?

*Attend and see if there be any sorrow
like unto my sorrow.*—Lam. 1:12.

Our Lord as He suffered felt really, and in his senses, that pain which is caused by some harmful bodily thing. He also felt that interior pain which is caused by the fear of something harmful and which we call sadness. In both these respects the pain suffered by Our Lord was the greatest pain possible in this present life. There are four reasons why this was so.

1. The causes of the pain.

The cause of the pain in the senses was the breaking up of the body, a pain whose bitterness derived partly from the fact that the sufferings attacked every part of His body, and partly from the fact that of all species of torture death by crucifixion is undoubtedly the most bitter. The nails are driven through the most sensitive of all places, the hands and the feet, the weight of the body itself increases the pain every moment. Add to this the long drawn-out agony, for the crucified do not die immediately as do those who are beheaded.

The cause of the internal pain was:

(i) All the sins of all mankind for which, by suffering, he was making satisfaction, so that, in a sense, he took them to him as though they were his own. "The words of my sins," it says in the Psalms (Ps. 21:2).

(ii) The special case of the Jews and the others who had had a share in the sin of his death, and especially the case of his disciples for whom his death had been a thing to be ashamed of.

(iii) The loss of his bodily life, which, by the nature of things, is something from which human nature turns away in horror.

2. We may consider the greatness of the pain according to the capacity, bodily and spiritual, for suffering of Him who suffered. In his body He was most admirably formed, for it was formed by the miraculous operation of the Holy Ghost, and therefore its sense of touch—that sense through which we experience pain—was of the keenest. His soul likewise, from its interior powers, had a knowledge as from experience of all the causes of sorrow.

3. The greatness of Our Lord's suffering can be considered in regard to this that the pain and sadness were without any alleviation. For in the case of no matter what other sufferer, the sadness of mind, and even the bodily pain, is lessened through a certain kind of reasoning, by means of which there is brought about a distraction of the sorrow from the higher powers to the lower. But when Our Lord suffered this did not happen, for he allowed each of his powers to act and suffer to the fullness of its special capacity.

4. We may consider the greatness of the suffering of Christ in the Passion in relation to this fact that the Passion and the pain it brought with it were deliberately undertaken by Christ with the object of freeing man from sin. And therefore he undertook to suffer an amount of pain proportionately equal to the extent of the fruit that was to follow from the Passion.

From all these causes, if we consider them together, it will be evident that the pain suffered by Christ was the greatest pain ever suffered.

(3.46.6.)

First Thursday

It Was Fitting that Christ Should Be Crucified with the Thieves

Christ was crucified between the thieves because such was the will of the Jews, and also because this was part of God's design. But the reasons why this was appointed were not the same in each of these cases.

1. As far as the Jews were concerned Our Lord was crucified with the thieves on either side to encourage the suspicion that he too was a criminal. But it fell out otherwise. The thieves themselves have left not a trace in the remembrance of man, while His cross is everywhere held in honor. Kings laying aside their crowns have broidered the cross on their royal robes. They have placed it on their crowns, on their arms. It has its place on the very altars. Everywhere, throughout the world, we behold the splendor of the cross.

In God's plan Christ was crucified with the thieves in order that, as for our sakes he became accursed of the cross, so, for our salvation, he is crucified like an evil thing among evil things.

2. The Pope St. Leo the Great says that the thieves were crucified, one on either side of him, so that in the very appearance of the scene of his suffering there might be set forth that distinction which should be made in the judgment of each one of us. St. Augustine has the same thought. "The cross itself," he says, "was a tribunal. In the center was the judge. To the one side a man who believed and was set free, to the other side a scoffer, and he was condemned." Already there was made clear the final fate of the living and the dead, the one class placed at his right, the other on his left.

3. According to St. Hilary the two thieves, placed to right and to left, typify that the whole of mankind is called to the mystery of Our Lord's Passion. And since division of things according to right and left is made with reference to believers and those who

will not believe, one of the two, placed on the right, is saved by justifying faith.

4. As St. Bede says, the thieves who were crucified with Our Lord, represent those who for the faith and to confess Christ undergo the agony of martyrdom or the severe discipline of a more perfect life. Those who do this for the sake of eternal glory are typified by the thief on the right hand. Those whose motive is the admiration of whoever beholds them imitate the spirit and the act of the thief on the left-hand side.

As Christ owed no debt in payment for which a man must die, but submitted to death of his own will, in order to overcome death, so also he had not done anything on account of which he deserved to be put with the thieves. But of his own will he chose to be reckoned among the wicked, that by his power he might destroy wickedness itself. Which is why St. John Chrysostom says that to convert the thief on the cross and to turn him to Paradise was as great a miracle as the earthquake.

(3.46.11.)

First Friday

THE FEAST OF THE HOLY LANCE
AND THE NAILS OF OUR LORD

One of the soldiers with a spear opened his side,
and immediately there came out blood and water.—John 19:34.

1. The gospel deliberately says "opened" and not "wounded" because through Our Lord's side there was opened to us the gate of eternal life. "After these things I looked, and behold a gate was opened in heaven" (Apoc. 4:1). This is the door opened in the ark, through which enter the animals who will not perish in the flood.

2. But this door is the cause of our salvation. "Immediately

there came forth blood and water," a thing truly miraculous, that, from a dead body, in which the blood congeals, blood should come forth.

This was done to show that by the Passion of Christ we receive a full absolution, an absolution from every sin and every stain. We receive this absolution from sin through that blood which is the price of our redemption. "You were not redeemed with corruptible things, as gold or silver, from your vain conversation with the tradition of your fathers; but with the precious blood of Christ, as of a lamb unspotted and undefiled" (1 Pet. 1:18).

We were absolved from every stain by the water, which is the laver of our redemption. In the prophet Ezekiel it is said, "I will pour upon you clean water, and you shall be cleaned from all your filthiness" (Ezek. 36:28), and in Zechariah, "There shall be a fountain open to the house of David and to the inhabitants of Jerusalem for the washing of the sinner and the unclean woman" (Zech. 13:1).

And so these two things may be thought of in relation to two of the sacraments, the water to baptism and the blood to the Holy Eucharist. Or both may be referred to the Holy Eucharist, since in the Mass water is mixed with the wine. Although the water is not of the substance of the sacrament.

Again, as from the side of Christ asleep in death on the cross there flowed that blood and water in which the Church is consecrated, so from the side of the sleeping Adam was formed the first woman, who herself foreshadowed the Church.

(In John 19.)

First Saturday

The Love of God Shown in the Passion of Christ

God commendeth his charity towards us: because when
as yet we were sinners, according to the time,
Christ died for us. —Rom. 5:8–9.

1. "Christ died for the ungodly" (*ibid.* 6) This is a great thing if we consider who it is that died, a great thing also if we consider on whose behalf he died. "For scarce for a just man, will one die" (*ibid.* 6), that is to say, that you will hardly find anyone who will die even to set free a man who is innocent; nay even it is said, "The just perisheth, and no man layeth it to heart" (Isaiah 57:1).

Rightly therefore does St. Paul say, "scarce will one die." There might perhaps be found one, some one rare person who out of superabundance of courage would be so bold as to die for a good man. But this is rare, for the simple reason that so to act is the greatest of all things. "Greater love than this no man hath," says Our Lord himself, "that a man lay down his life for his friends" (John 15:13).

But the like of what Christ did himself, to die for evildoers and the wicked, has never been seen. Wherefore rightly do we ask in wonderment why Christ did it.

2. If in fact it be asked why Christ died for the wicked, the answer is that God in this way "commendeth his charity towards us." He shows us in this way that He loves us with a love that knows no limits, "for while we were as yet sinners Christ died for us."

The very death of Christ for us shows the love of God, for it was His son whom He gave to die, that satisfaction might be made for us. "God so loved the world, as to give His only begotten Son" (John 3:16). And thus as the love of God the Father for us is shown in his giving us His Holy Spirit, so also is it shown in this way, by his gift of his only Son.

The Apostle says God "commendeth," signifying thereby that the love of God is a thing which cannot be measured. This is shown by the very fact of the matter, namely, the fact that he gave His Son to die for us, and it is shown also by reason of the kind of people we are for whom He died. Christ was not stirred up to die for us by any merits of ours, "when as yet we were sinners." "God (who is rich in mercy) for his exceeding charity wherewith he loved us, even when we were dead in sins, hath quickened us together in Christ" (Eph. 2:4).   *(In Rom. 5.)*

3. All these things are almost too much to be believed. "A work is done in your days, which no man will believe when it shall be told" (Habak. 1:5). This truth that Christ died for us is so hard a truth that scarcely can our intelligence take hold of it. Nay it is a truth that our intelligence could in no way discover, And St. Paul, preaching, makes echo to Habakkuk, "I work a work in your days, a work which you will not believe, if any man shall tell it to you" (Acts 13:14).

So great is God's love for us and his grace toward us, that he does more for us than we can believe or understand.

(In Symbolum.)

Second Week in Lent—Sunday

GOD THE FATHER DELIVERED CHRIST TO HIS PASSION

God spared not even His own Son,
but delivered Him up for us all.—Rom. 8:32.

Christ suffered willingly, moved by obedience to His Father. Wherefore, God the Father delivered Christ to his Passion, and this in three ways:

1. Because the Father, of His eternal will, preordained the Passion of Christ as the means whereby to free the human race. So

it is said in Isaiah, "The Lord hath laid on Him the iniquity of us all: (Isa. 53:6), and again, "The Lord was pleased to bruise him in infirmity" (Isa. 53:10).

2. Because He inspired Our Lord with the willingness to suffer for us, pouring into his soul the love which produced the will to suffer. Whence the prophet goes on to say, "He was offered because it was his own will" (Isa. 53:7).

3. Because He did not protect Our Lord from the Passion, but exposed him to his persecutors. Whence we read in St. Matthew's Gospel, that as he hung on the cross Christ said, "My God, my God, why hast thou forsaken me" (Matt. 27:46). For God the Father, that is to say, had left him at the mercy of his torturers.

To hand over an innocent man to suffering and to death, against his will, compelling him to die as it were, would indeed be cruel and wicked. But it was not in this way that God the Father handed over Christ. He handed over Christ by inspiring Him with the will to suffer for us. By so doing, the severity of God is made clear to us, that no sin is forgiven without punishment undergone, which St. Paul again teaches when he says, "God spared not his own Son."

At the same time, God's good-heartedness is shown in the fact that whereas man could not, no matter what his punishment, sufficiently make satisfaction, God has given man someone who can make that satisfaction for him. Which is what St. Paul means by, "He delivered him up for us all," and again when he says, "God hath proposed Christ to be a propitiation, through faith in his blood" (Rom. 3:25).

The same activity in a good man and in a bad man is differently judged inasmuch as the root from which it proceeds is different. The Father, for example, delivered over Christ and Christ delivered himself, and this from love, and therefore They are praised. Judas delivered Him from love of gain, the Jews from hatred, Pilate from the worldly fear with which he feared Caesar, and these are rightly regarded with horror.   (3.47.3.)

Christ therefore did not owe to death the debt of necessity, but of charity the charity to men by which he willed their salvation, and the charity to God by which he willed to fulfill God's will, as it says in the gospel, "Not as I will but as Thou wilt" (Matt. 26:39).

(2 Dist. 20.1.5.)

Second Monday

IT WAS FITTING THAT OUR LORD SHOULD SUFFER AT THE HANDS OF THE GENTILES

They shall deliver him to the Gentiles, to be mocked, and scourged, and crucified.—Matt. 20:19.

In the very manner of the Passion of Our Lord its effects are foreshadowed. In the first place, the Passion of Our Lord had for its effect the salvation of Jews, many of whom were baptized in his death.

Secondly, by the preaching of these Jews, the effects of the Passion passed to the Gentiles also. There was thus a certain fitness in Our Lord's Passion beginning with the Jews and then, the Jews handing him on, that it should be completed at the hands of the Gentiles.

To show the abundance of the love which moved him to suffer, Christ, on the very cross, asked mercy for his tormentors. And since He wished that Jew and Gentile alike should realize this truth about His love, so he wished that both should have a share in making him suffer.

It was the Jews and not the Gentiles who offered the figurative sacrifices of the Old Law. The Passion of Christ was an offering through sacrifice, inasmuch as Christ underwent death by his own will moved by charity. But in so far as those who put him to death were concerned, they were not offering a sacrifice but committing a sin.

When the Jews declared, "It is not lawful for us to put any man to death" (John 19:31), they may have had many things in mind. It was not lawful for them to put anyone to death on account of the holiness of the feast they had begun to keep. Perhaps they wished Christ to be killed not as a transgressor of their own law but as an enemy of the state, because he had made himself a king, a charge concerning which they had no jurisdiction. Or again, they may have meant that they had no power to crucify which was what they longed for but only to stone, as they later stoned St. Stephen. Or, the most likely thing of all, that their Roman conquerors had taken away their power of life and death.

(3.47.4.)

Second Tuesday

THE PASSION OF CHRIST BROUGHT ABOUT OUR SALVATION BECAUSE IT WAS A MERITORIOUS ACT

1. Grace was given to Christ not only as to a particular person, but also as far as he is the head of the Church, in order that the grace might pass over from him to his members.

And the good works Christ performed, therefore, stand in this same way in relation to him and to his members, as the good works of any other man in a state of grace stand to himself.

Now it is evident that any man who, in a state of grace, suffers for justice' sake, merits for himself, by this very fact alone, salvation. As is said in the gospel, "Blessed are they that suffer persecution for justice' sake" (Matt. 5:10).

Whence Christ by his Passion merited salvation not only for himself but for all his members.

Christ, indeed, from the very instant of his conception, merited eternal salvation for us. But there still remained certain obstacles on our part, obstacles which kept us from possessing our selves of the effect of what Christ had merited. Wherefore, in order to remove these obstacles, "It behooved Christ to suffer" (Luke 24:46).

Now although the love of Christ for us was not increased in the Passion, and was not greater in the Passion than before it, the Passion of Christ had a certain effect which His previous meritorious activity did not have. The Passion produced this effect not on account of any greater love shown thereby, but because it was a kind of action fitted to produce that effect, as is evident from what has been said already on the fitness of the Passion of Christ.

(3.48.1.)

Head and members belong to one and the same person. Now Christ is our head, according to his divinity and to the fullness of his grace which overflows upon others also. We are his members. What Christ then meritoriously acquires is not something external and foreign to us, but, by virtue of the unity of the mystical body, it over flows upon us too.

(3 Dist. 18.6).

2. We should know, too, that although Christ by his death acquired merit sufficient for the whole human race, there are special things needed for the particular salvation of each individual soul, and these each soul must itself seek out. The death of Christ is, as it were, the cause of all salvation, as the sin of the first man was the cause of all condemnation. But if each individual man is to share in the effect of a universal cause, the universal cause needs to be specially applied to each individual man.

Now the effect of the sin of the first parents is transmitted to each individual through his bodily origin (i.e., through his being a bodily descendant of the first man). The effect of the death of Christ is transmitted to each man through a spiritual rebirth, a rebirth in which man is, as it were, conjoined with Christ and incorporated with him.

Therefore it is that each individual must seek to be born again

through Christ, and to receive those other things in which works
the power of the death of Christ.

(Contra Gen. 4.55.)

Second Wednesday

THE PASSION OF CHRIST BROUGHT ABOUT OUR SALVATION BECAUSE IT WAS AN ACT OF SATISFACTION

*He is the propitiation for our sins, and not for ours only
but also for those of the whole world.*—1 John 2:2.

1. Satisfaction for offenses committed is truly made when there is
offered to the person offended a thing which he loves as much as,
or more than, he hates the offenses committed.

Christ, however, by suffering out of love and out of obedience,
offered to God something greater by far than the satisfaction called
for by all the sins of all mankind, and this for three reasons. In the
first place, there was the greatness of the love which moved him
to suffer. Then there was the worth of the life which he laid down
in satisfaction, the life of God and man. Finally, on account of the
way in which his Passion involved every part of his being, and of
the greatness of the suffering he undertook.

So it is that the Passion of Christ was not merely sufficient
but superabundant as a satisfaction for men's sins. It would seem
indeed to be the case that satisfaction should be made by the person
who committed the offense. But head and members are as it were
one mystical person, and therefore the satisfaction made by Christ
avails all the faithful as they are the members of Christ. One man
can always make satisfaction for another, so long as the two are
one in charity.   *(3.48.2.)*

2. Although Christ, by his death, made sufficient satisfaction
for original sin, it is not unfitting that the penal consequences

of original sin should still remain even in those who are made sharers in Christ's redemption. This has been done fittingly and usefully, so that the penalties remain even though the guilt has been removed.

(i) It has been done so that there might be conformity between the faithful and Christ, as there is conformity between members and head. Just as Christ first of all suffered many pains and came in this way to his glory, so it is only right that his faithful should also first be subjected to sufferings and thence enter into immortality, themselves bearing as it were the livery of the Passion of Christ so as to enjoy a glory somewhat like to his.

(ii) A second reason is that if men coming to Christ were straightway freed from suffering and the necessity of death, only too many would come to him attracted rather by these temporal advantages than by spiritual things. And this would be altogether contrary to the intention of Christ, who came into this world that he might convert men from a love of temporal advantages and win them to spiritual things.

(iii) Finally, if those who came to Christ were straightway rendered immortal and impassible, this would in a kind of way compel men to receive the faith of Christ, and so the merit of believing would be lessened.

(Contra Gen. 4.55.)

Second Thursday

That the Passion of Christ Brought about Its Effect Because It Was a Sacrifice

1. A sacrifice properly so called is something done to render God the honor specially due to Him, in order to appease Him. St. Augustine teaches this, saying, "Every work done in order that we may,

in a holy union, cleave to God is a true sacrifice every work, that is to say, related to that final good whose possession alone can make us truly happy." Christ in the Passion offered himself for us, and it was just this circumstance that he offered himself willingly which was to God the most precious thing of all, since the willingness came from the greatest possible love. Whence it is evident that the Passion of Christ was a real sacrifice.

And as he himself adds later. The former sacrifices of the saints were so many signs, of different kinds, of this one true sacrifice. This one thing was signified through many things, as one thing is said through many words, so that it may be repeated often without beginning to weary people.

St. Augustine speaks of four things being found in every sacrifice, namely, a person to whom the offering is made; one by whom it is made; the thing offered; and those on whose behalf it is offered. These are all found in the Passion of Our Lord. It is the same person, the only, true mediator himself, who through the sacrifice of peace reconciles us to God, yet remains one with him to whom he offers, who makes one with him those for whom he offers, and is himself one who both offers and is offered.

2. It is true that in those sacrifices of the old law which were types of Christ, human flesh was never offered, but it does not follow from this that the Passion of Christ was not a sacrifice. For although the reality and the thing that typifies it must coincide in one point, it is not necessary that they coincide in every point, for the reality must go beyond the thing that typifies it. It was then very fitting that the sacrifice in which the flesh of Christ is offered for us was typified by a sacrifice not of the flesh of man but of other animals, to foreshadow the flesh of Christ which is the most perfect sacrifice of all. It is the most perfect sacrifice of all.

(i) Because since it is the flesh of human nature that is offered, it is a thing fittingly offered for men and fittingly received by men in a sacrament.

(ii) Because, since the flesh of Christ was able to suffer and to die it was suitable for immolation.

(iii) Because since that flesh was itself without sin, it had a power to cleanse from sin.

(iv) Because being the flesh of the very offerer, it was acceptable to God by reason of the unspeakable love of the one who was offering his own flesh.

Whence St. Augustine says: "What is there more suitably received by men, of offerings made on their behalf, than human flesh, and what is so suitable for immolation as mortal flesh? And what is so clean for cleansing mortal viciousness as that flesh born, without stain of carnal desire, in the womb and of the womb of a virgin? And what can be so graciously offered and received as the flesh of our sacrifice, the body so produced of our priest?"

(3.48.3.)

Second Friday

FEAST OF THE HOLY WINDING SHEET

Joseph taking the body, wrapped it up in a clean linen cloth and laid it in his own new monument.—Matt. 27:59.

1. By this clean linen cloth three things are signified in a hidden way, namely:

(i) The pure body of Christ. For the cloth was made of linen which by much pressing is made white, and in like manner it was after much pressure that the body of Christ came to the brightness of the resurrection. "Thus it behooved Christ to suffer, and to rise again from the dead the third day" (Luke 24:46).

(ii) The Church, which "without spot or wrinkle" (Eph. 5:27), is signified by this linen woven out of many threads.

(iii) A clear conscience, where Christ reposes.

2. "And laid him in his own new monument."

It was Joseph's own grave, and certainly it was somehow appropriate that he who had died for the sins of others should be buried in another man's grave.

Notice that it was a new grave. Had other bodies already been laid in it, there might have been a doubt which had arisen. There is another fitness in this circumstance, namely that he who was buried in this new grave, was he who was born of a virgin mother.

As Mary's womb knew no child before him nor after him, so was it with this grave. Again we may understand that it is in a soul renewed that Christ is buried by faith, that Christ may dwell by faith in our hearts (Eph. 3:17).

St. John's Gospel adds, "Now there was in the place where he was crucified, a garden; and in the garden a new sepulcher" (John 10:41). Which recalls to us that as Christ was taken in a garden and suffered his agony in a garden, so in a garden was he buried, and thereby we are reminded that it was from the sin committed by Adam in the garden of delightfulness that, by the power of his Passion, Christ set us free, and also that through the Passion the Church was consecrated, the Church which again is as a garden closed.

(In Matt. 26.)

Second Saturday

The Passion of Christ Wrought Our Salvation by Redeeming Us

St. Peter says, "You were not redeemed with corruptible things, as gold or silver, from your vain conversation of the tradition of your fathers: but with the precious blood of Christ, as of a lamb unspotted and undefiled" (1 Pet. 1:18).

St. Paul says, "Christ hath redeemed us from the curse of the law, being made a curse for us" (Gal. 3:13). He is said to be accursed in our place inasmuch as it was for us that he suffered on the cross. Therefore by his Passion he redeemed us.

Sin, in fact, had bound man with a double obligation.

(i) An obligation that made him sin's slave. For Jesus said, "Whosoever committeth sin is the servant of sin" (John 8:34). A man is enslaved to whoever overcomes him. Therefore since the devil, in inducing man to sin, had overcome man, man was bound in servitude to the devil.

(ii) A further obligation existed, namely between man and the penalty due for the sin committed, and man was bound in this way in accord with the justice of God. This, too, was a kind of servitude, for to servitude or slavery it belongs that a man must suffer otherwise than he chooses, since the free man is the man who uses himself as he wills.

Since then the Passion of Christ made sufficient, and more than sufficient, satisfaction for the sins of all mankind and for the penalty due to them, the Passion was a kind of price through which we were free from both these obligations. For the satisfaction itself—that by means of which one makes satisfaction, whether for oneself or for another—is spoken of as a kind of price by which one redeems or buys back oneself or another from sin and from merited penalties. So in Holy Scripture it is said, "Redeem thou thy sins with alms" (Dan. 4:24).

Christ made satisfaction not indeed by a gift of money or anything of that sort, but by a gift that was the greatest of all, by giving for us Himself. And thus it is that the Passion of Christ is called our redemption.

By sinning man bound himself not to God but to the devil. As far as concerns the guilt of what he did, he had offended God and had made him self subject to the devil, assenting to his will.

Hence he did not, by reason of the sin committed, bind himself to God, but rather, deserting God's service, he had fallen under the yoke of the devil. And God, with justice if we remember the offense committed against Him, had not prevented this.

But, if we consider the matter of the punishment earned, it was chiefly and in the first place to God that man was bound, as to the supreme judge. Man was, in respect of punishment, bound to the devil only in a lesser sense, as to the torturer, as it says in the gospel, "Lest the adversary deliver thee to the judge, and the judge deliver thee to the officer" (Matt. 5:25), that is, to the cruel minister of punishments.

Therefore, although the devil unjustly, as far as was in his power, held man—whom by his lies he had deceived—bound in slavery, held him bound both on account of the guilt and of the punishment due for it, it was nevertheless just that man should suffer in this way. The slavery which he suffered on account of the thing done God did not prevent, and the slavery he suffered as punishment God decreed.

Therefore it was in regard to God's claims that justice called for man to be redeemed, and not in regard to the devil's hold on us. And it was to God the price was paid and not to the devil.

(3.48.4.)

Third Week in Lent—Sunday

IT IS THE PASSION OF CHRIST THAT HAS FREED US FROM SIN

He hath loved us, and washed us from our sins in his own blood.—Apoc. 1:5.

The Passion of Christ is the proper cause of the remission of our sins, and that in three ways.

1. Because it provokes us to love God. St. Paul says, "God

commendeth his charity towards us; because when as yet we were sinners, Christ died for us" (Rom. 5:8).

Through charity we obtain forgiveness for sin, as it says in the gospel: "Many sins are forgiven her, because she hath loved much" (Luke 7:47).

2. The Passion of Christ is the cause of the forgiveness of sins because it is an act of redemption. Since Christ is himself our head, he has, by his own Passion undertaken from love and obedience delivered us his members from our sins, as it were at the price of his Passion. Just as a man might by some act of goodness done with his hands buy himself off for a wrong thing he had done with his feet. For as man's natural body is a unity, made up of different limbs, so the whole Church, which is the mystical body of Christ, is reckoned as a single person with its own head, and this head is Christ.

3. The Passion of Christ was a thing equal to its task. For the human nature through which Christ suffered his Passion is the instrument of His divine nature. Whence all the actions and all the sufferings of that human nature wrought to drive out sin are wrought by a power that is divine.

Christ, in His Passion, delivered us from our sins in a causal way, that is to say, he set up for us a thing which would be a cause of our emancipation, a thing whereby any sin might at any time be remitted, whether committed now, or in times gone by, or in time to come: much as a physician might make a medicine from which all who are sick may be healed, even those sick in the years yet to come.

But since what gives the Passion of Christ its excellence is the fact that it is the universal cause of the forgiveness of sins, it is necessary that we each of us ourselves make use of it for the forgiveness of our own particular sins. This is done through Baptism, Penance and the other sacraments, whose power derives from the Passion of Christ.

By faith also we make use of the Passion of Christ, in order to receive its fruits, as St. Paul says: "Christ Jesus, whom God hath proposed to be a propitiation, through faith in his blood" (Rom. 3:25). But the faith by which we are cleansed from sin is not that faith which can exist side by side with sin—the faith called formless—but faith formed, that is to say, faith made alive by charity. So that the Passion of Christ is not through faith applied merely to our understanding but also to our will. Again, it is from the power of the Passion of Christ that the sins are forgiven which are forgiven by faith in this way.

(3.49.1.)

Third Monday

The Passion of Christ
Has Delivered Us from the Devil

Our Lord said, as His Passion drew near: "Now shall the princes of this world be cast out. And I, if I be lifted up from the earth, will draw all things to myself" (John 12:31–32).

He was lifted up from the earth by His Passion on the cross. Therefore by that Passion the devil was driven out from his dominion over men.

With reference to that power, which, before the Passion of Christ, the devil used to exercise over mankind, three things are to be borne in mind.

1. Man had by his sin earned for himself enslavement to the devil, for it was by the devil's temptation that he had been overcome.

2. God, whom man in sinning had offended, had, by his justice, abandoned man to the enslavement of the devil.

3. The devil by his own most wicked will stood in the way of man's achieving his salvation.

With regard to the first point, the Passion of Christ set man free from the devil's power because the Passion of Christ brought about the forgiveness of sin. As to the second point, the Passion delivered man from the devil because it brought about a reconciliation between God and man. As to the third point, the Passion of Christ freed us from the devil's power because in his action during the Passion the devil over-reached himself. He went beyond the limits of the power over men allowed to him by God, when he plotted the death of Christ, upon whom, since he was without sin, there lay no debt payable by death. Whence St. Augustine's words: "The devil was overcome by the justice of Christ. In Him the devil found nothing that deserved death, but, none the less, he slew him. And it was but just that those debtors that the devil detained should go free since they believed in Him whom, though he was under no bond to him, the devil had slain."

The devil still continues to exercise a power over men. He can, God permitting it, tempt them in soul and in body. There is, however, made available for man a remedy in the Passion of Christ, by means of which he can defend himself against these attacks, so that they do not lead him into the destruction of eternal death. Likewise all those who before the Passion of Christ resisted the devil had derived their power to resist from the Passion, although the Passion had not yet been accomplished. But in one point none of those who lived before the Passion had been able to escape the hand of the devil, namely, they all had to go down into hell, a thing from which, since the Passion, all men can, by his power, defend themselves.

God also allows the devil to deceive men in certain persons, times and places, according to the hidden character of His designs. Such, for example, will be anti-Christ. But there always remains, and for the age of anti-Christ too, a remedy prepared for man through the Passion of Christ, a power of protecting himself against the wickedness of the devils. The fact that there are some who neglect to make use of this remedy does not lessen the efficacy of the Passion of Christ. *(3.49.2)*

Third Tuesday

CHRIST IS TRULY OUR REDEEMER

You were redeemed with the precious blood of Christ,
as of a lamb unspotted and undefiled.—1 Pet. 1:19.

By the sin of our first parents, the whole human race was alienated from God, as is taught in the second chapter of the epistle to the Ephesians. It was not from God's power that we were thereby cut off, but from that sight of God's face to which His children and His servants are admitted.

Then again we descended beneath the usurped power of the devil. Man had consented to the devil's will and, thereby, had made himself subject to the devil—subject, that is to say, as far as lay in man's power, for since he was not his own property, but the property of another, he could not really give himself away to the devil.

By His Passion, then, Christ did two things. He freed us from the power of the enemy, conquering him by virtues which were the very contraries to the vices by which he had conquered man—by humility, namely, by obedience, and by an austerity of suffering that was in direct opposition to the enjoyment of forbidden food.

Furthermore, by making satisfaction for the sin committed, Christ joined man with God and made him the child and servant of God.

This emancipation had about it two things that make it a kind of buying. Christ is said to have bought us back or to have redeemed us inasmuch as he snatched us from the power of the devil, as a king is said, by hard-fought battles, to redeem his kingdom that the enemy has occupied. Christ is again said to have redeemed us inasmuch as He placated God for us, paying as it were the price of His satisfaction on our behalf, that we might be freed both from the penalty and from the sin.

This price, His precious blood, he paid that he might make satisfaction for us not to the devil, but to God. Again, by the victory that His Passion was, he took us away from the devil. The devil had indeed had dominion over us, but unjustly, since what power he had was usurped. Nevertheless, it was but just that we should fall under his yoke, seeing that it was by him we were overcome. This is why it was necessary that the devil should be overcome by the very contrary of the forces by which he had himself overcome. For he had not overcome by violence, but by a lying persuasion to sin.

(3 Dist. 19.91, a 4.)

Third Wednesday

THE PRICE OF OUR REDEMPTION

You are bought with a great price.—1 Cor. 6:20.

The indignities and sufferings anyone suffers are measured according to the dignity of the person concerned. If a king is struck in the face, he suffers a greater indignity than does a private person. But the dignity of Christ is infinite, for He is a divine person. Therefore, any suffering undergone by him, even the least conceivable suffering, is infinite. Any suffering at all, then, undergone by Him, without His death, would have sufficed to redeem the human race.

St. Bernard says that the least drop of the blood of Christ would have sufficed for the redemption of us all. And Christ could have shed that one drop without dying. Therefore, even without dying he could, by some kind of suffering, have redeemed, that is, bought back, all mankind.

Now in buying two things are required: an amount equal to the price demanded, and the assigning of that amount to the purpose of buying. For if a man gives a price that is not equal in value to the thing to be bought, we do not say that he has bought it, but only that he has partly bought it, and partly been given it. For example, if a man buys for ten dollars a book that is worth twenty dollars, he has partly bought the book and it has, partly, been given to him. Or again, if he puts together a greater price but does not assign it to the buying, he is not said to buy the book.

If therefore when we speak of the redemption and buying back of the human race, we have in view the amount of the price. We must say that any suffering undergone by Christ, even without His death, would have sufficed because of the infinite worth of His person. If, however, we speak of the redemption with reference to the setting of the price to the purpose in hand, we have then to say that no other suffering of Christ less than His death, was set by God and by Christ as the price to be paid for the redemption of mankind. And this was so for three reasons:

1. That the price of our redemption should not only be infinite in value, but be of the same kind as what it bought, i.e., that it should be with a death that He bought us back from death.

2. That the death of Christ would be not only the price of our redemption but also an example of courage, so that men would not be afraid to die for the truth. St. Paul makes mention of this and the preceding cause when he says: "That, through death, he might destroy him who had the empire of death," (this is the first cause), "and might deliver them, who through the fear of death were all their lifetime subject to servitude" (this for the second cause) (Heb. 2:14–15).

3. That the death of Christ might be a sacrament to work our salvation; we, that is, dying to sin, to bodily desires, and to our own will through the power of the death of Christ. These reasons are given by St. Peter when he says, "Christ who died once for our sins,

the just for the unjust; that he might offer us to God, being put to death indeed in the flesh, but enlivened in the spirit" (1 Pet. 3:18).

And so it is that mankind has not been redeemed by any other suffering of Christ without his death.

But, as a matter of fact, Christ would have paid sufficiently for the redemption of mankind not only by giving His own life, but by suffering any suffering, no matter how slight, if this slight suffering had been the thing divinely appointed, and Christ would thereby have paid sufficiently because of the infinite worth of His person.

(Quodlib. 2 q 1, a 2.)

Third Thursday

THE PREACHING OF THE SAMARITAN WOMAN

The woman therefore left her water-pot,
and went her way into the city.—John 4:28.

This woman, once Christ had instructed her, became an apostle. There are three things which we can gather from what she said and what she did.

1. The entirety of her surrender to Our Lord. This is shown:

(i) From the fact that she left lying there, almost as if forgotten, that for which she had come to the well, the water and the water-pot. So great was her absorption. Hence it is said, "The woman left her water-pot and went away into the city"—went away to announce the wonderful works of Christ. She cared no longer for the bodily comforts in view of the usefulness of better things, following in this the example of the Apostles of whom it is said that, "Leaving their nets, they followed the Lord" (Mark 1:18).

The water-pot stands for fashionable desire, by means of which men draw up pleasures from those depths of darkness signified by the well, that is, from practices which are of the earth earthy. Those who abandon such desires for the sake of God are like the woman who left her water-pot.

(ii) From the multitude of people to whom she tells the news, not to one nor to two or three, but to a whole city. This is why she "went away into the city."

2. A method of preaching.

"She saith to the men there: Come, and see a man who has told me all things whatsoever I have done. Is not he the Christ?" (John 4:29).

(i) She invites them to look upon Christ: "Come, and see a man." She did not straightway say that they should give themselves to Christ, for that might have been for them an occasion for blasphemy, but, to begin with, she told them things about Christ which were believable and open to observation. She told them he was a man. Nor did she say, "Believe, but come and see," for she knew that if they, too, tasted of that well, looking that is upon Our Lord, they, too, would feel all she had felt. And she follows the example of a true preacher in that she attracts the men not to herself but to Christ.

(ii) She gives them a hint that Christ is God when she says, "A man who has told me all things whatsoever I have done"—that is to say, how many husbands she had had. She is not ashamed to bring up things that make for her own confusion because the soul, once it is lighted up with the divine fire, in no way looks to earthly values and standards, cares neither for its own glory nor its shame, but only for that flame which holds and consumes it.

(iii) She suggests that this proves the majesty of Christ, saying, "Is not he the Christ?" She does not dare to assert that he is the Christ, lest she have the appearance of wishing to teach others, and the others, irritated thereat, refuse to go out to Him. Nor, on the other hand, does she leave the matter in silence, but she puts it before them questioningly, as though she left it to their own judgment. For this is the easiest of all ways of persuasion.

3. The Fruit of Preaching.

"They therefore went out of the city, and came unto Christ" (John 4:30).

Hereby it is made clear to us that if we would come to Christ, we too must go out of the city, which is to say, we must lay aside all love of bodily delights.

"Let us go forth therefore to him without the camp" (Heb. 13:13).

(In John 4.)

Third Friday

IT IS BY THE PASSION OF CHRIST THAT WE HAVE BEEN FREED FROM THE PUNISHMENT DUE TO SIN

Surely he hath borne our infirmities
and carried our sorrows. —Isaiah 53:4.

By the Passion of Christ we are freed from the liability to be punished for sin with the punishment that sin calls for in two ways, directly and indirectly.

We are freed *directly* inasmuch as the Passion of Christ made sufficient and more than sufficient satisfaction for the sins of the whole human race. Now once sufficient satisfaction has been made, the liability to the punishment mentioned is destroyed.

We are freed *indirectly* inasmuch as the Passion of Christ causes the sin to be remitted, and it is from the sin that the liability to the punishment mentioned derives.

Souls in hell, however, are not freed by the Passion of Christ, because the Passion of Christ shares its effect with those to whom it is applied by faith and by charity and by the sacraments of faith. Therefore the souls in hell, who are not linked up with the Passion of Christ in the way just mentioned, cannot receive its effects.

Now although we are freed from liability to the precise penalty that sin deserves, there is, nevertheless, enjoined on the repentant sinner a penalty or penance of satisfaction. For in order that the effect of the Passion of Christ be fully worked out in us, it is necessary for us to be made of like form with Christ. Now we are made of like form with Christ in baptism by the sacrament, as is said by St. Paul, "We are buried together with him by baptism into death" (Rom. 6:4). Whence it is that no penalty of satisfaction is imposed on those who are baptized. Through the satisfaction made by Christ they are wholly set free. But since "Christ died once for our sins" (1 Pet. 3:18), once only, man cannot a second time be made of like form with the death of Christ through the sacrament of baptism. Therefore those who, after baptism, sin again, must be made like to Christ in his suffering, through some kind of penalty or suffering which they endure in their own persons.

If death, which is a penalty due to sin, continues to subsist, the reason is this: The satisfaction made by Christ produces its effect in us in so far as we are made of one body with him, in the way limbs are one body with the head. Now it is necessary that the limbs be made to conform to the head. Wherefore since Christ at first had, together with the grace in his soul, a liability to suffer in his body, and came to His glorious immortality through the Passion, so also should it be with us, who are his limbs. By the Passion we are indeed delivered from any punishment as a thing fixed on us, but we are delivered in such a way that it is in the soul we first receive the spirit of the adoption of sons, by which we are put on the list for the inheritance of eternal glory, while we still retain a body that can suffer and die. It is only afterward, when we have been fashioned to the likeness of Christ in his sufferings and death, that we are brought into the glory of immortality. St. Paul teaches this when he says: "If sons, heirs also; heirs indeed of God, and joint heirs with Christ: yet so, if we suffer with him, that we may be also glorified with him (Rom. 8:17).   (3.49.3.)

Third Saturday

THE PASSION OF CHRIST RECONCILES US TO GOD

We were reconciled to God
through the death of his son.—Rom. 5:10.

1. The Passion of Christ brought about our reconciliation to God in two ways.

It removed the sin that had made the human race God's enemy, as it says in Holy Scripture: "To God the wicked and his wickedness are alike hateful" (Wis. 14:9), and again, "Thou hatest all the workers of iniquity" (Ps. 5:7).

Secondly, the Passion was a sacrifice most acceptable to God. It is in fact the peculiar effect of sacrifice to be itself a thing by which God is placated: just as a man remits offenses done against him for the sake of some acknowledgment, pleasing to him, which is made. Whence it is said, "If the Lord stir thee up against me, let him accept of sacrifice" (1 Samuel 26:19). Likewise, the voluntary suffering of Christ was so good a thing in itself, that for the sake of this good thing found in human nature, God was pleased beyond the totality of offenses committed by all mankind, as far as concerns all those who are linked to Christ in his suffering by faith and by charity.

When we say that the Passion of Christ reconciled us to God we do not mean that God began to love us all over again, for it is written, "I have loved thee with an everlasting love" (Jer. 31:3). We mean that by the Passion the cause of the hatred was taken away, on the one hand by the removal of the sin, on the other hand by the compensation of a good that was more than acceptable.

(3.49.4.)

2. As far as those who slew Our Lord were concerned the Passion was indeed a cause of wrath. But the love of Christ suffering was greater than the wickedness of those who caused Him to suffer. And therefore the Passion of Christ was more powerful in

reconciling to God the whole human race, than in moving God to anger.

God's love for us is shown by what it does for us. God is said to love some men because he gives them a share in His own goodness, in that vision of His very essence from which there follows this—that we live with Him, in His company, as His friends, for it is in that delightful condition of things that happiness (beatitude) consists.

God is then said to love those whom He admits to that vision, either by giving them the vision directly or by giving them what will bring them to the vision as when he gives the Holy Spirit as a pledge of the vision.

It was from this sharing in the divine goodness, from this vision of God's very essence, that man, by sin, had been removed, and it is in this sense that we speak of man as deprived of God's love.

And inasmuch as Christ, making satisfaction for us by His Passion, brought it about that men were admitted to the vision of God, therefore it is that Christ is said to have reconciled us to God.

(2 Dist. 19 q 1, a 5.)

Fourth Week in Lent—Sunday

CHRIST BY HIS PASSION
OPENED TO US THE GATES OF HEAVEN

We have a confidence in the entering into the holies by the blood of Christ.—Heb. 10:19.

The closing of a gate is an obstacle hindering men's entrance. Now men are hindered from entrance to the heavenly kingdom by sin, for Isaiah says, "It shall be called the holy way: the unclean shall not pass over it" (Is. 35:8).

Now the sin that hinders man's entrance into heaven is of two kinds. There is, first of all, the sin of our first parents. By this sin access to the kingdom of heaven was barred to man. We read in Genesis (3:24) that after the sin of our first parents God "placed before the paradise of pleasure Cherubims and a flaming sword, turning every way, to keep the way of the tree of life." The other kind of hindrance arises from the sins special to each individual, the sins each man commits by his own particular action.

By the Passion of Christ we are freed not only from the sin common to all human nature, and this both as to the sin and as to its appointed penalty, since Christ pays the price on our behalf, but also we are delivered from our personal sins if we are numbered among those who are linked to the Passion by faith, by charity, and by the sacraments of the Faith. Thus it is that through the Passion of Christ the gates of heaven are thrown open to us. And hence St. Paul says that "Christ, being come an high priest of the good things to come, by his own blood entered once into the holies, having obtained a redemption that is eternal" (Heb. 9:11).

And this was foreshadowed in the Old Testament, where we read (Num. 35:25, 28), "the man-slayer shall abide there," that is, in the city of refuge, "until the death of the high priest, that is anointed with holy oil. And after he is dead, then shall the man-slayer return to his own country."

The holy fathers who (before the coming of Christ) wrought works of justice earned their entrance into heaven through faith in the Passion of Christ, as is written: "The saints by faith conquered kingdoms, wrought justice" (Heb. 11:33). By faith, too, it was that individuals were cleansed from the sins they had individually committed. But faith or goodness, no matter who the person was that possessed it, was not enough to be able to move the hindrance created by the guilty state of the whole human creation. This hindrance was only removed at the price of the blood of Christ. And therefore before the Passion of Christ no one could enter the heavenly kingdom, to obtain that eternal happiness that consists in the full enjoyment of God.

Christ by his Passion merited for us an entrance into heaven, and removed what stood in our way. By His Ascension, however, he, as it were, put mankind in possession of heaven. And therefore it is that He ascended opening the way before them.   *(3.49.5.)*

Fourth Monday

Christ by His Passion Merited to Be Exalted

He became obedient unto death, even to the death of the cross: for which cause God hath exalted him.—Phil. 2:8.

Merit is a thing which implies a certain equality of justice. Thus St. Paul says, "To him that worketh, the reward is reckoned according to debt" (Rom. 4:4).

Now since a man who commits an injustice takes for himself more than is due to himself, it is just that he suffer loss even in what is actually due to him. If a man steals one sheep, he shall give back four, as it says in Holy Scripture (Exod. 22:1). And this is said to be merited inasmuch as in this way the man's evil will is punished. In the same way the man who acts with such justice that he take less than what is due to him, merits that more shall be generously superadded to what he has, as a kind of reward for his just will. So, for instance, the gospel tells us, "He that humbleth himself shall be exalted" (Luke 14:11).

Now in His Passion Christ humbled himself below His dignity in four respects:

(i) In respect of His Passion and His death, things which He did not owe to undergo.

(ii) In respect to places, for His body was placed in a grave and his soul in hell.

(iii) In respect to the confusion and shame that He endured.

(iv) In respect to His being delivered over to human authority, as He said Himself to Pilate, "Thou shouldst not have any power against me, unless it were given thee from above" (John 19:11).

Therefore, on account of His Passion, He merited a fourfold exaltation.

(i) A glorious resurrection. It is said in the Psalm (Ps. 138:1), "Thou hast known my sitting down," that is, the humiliation of my Passion, "and my rising up."

(ii) An ascension into heaven. Whence it is said, "He descended first into the lower parts of the earth: He that descended is the same also that ascended above all the heavens" (Eph. 4:9–10).

(iii) To be seated at the right hand of the Father, with His divinity made manifest. Isaiah (52:13) says, "He shall be exalted, and extolled, and shall be exceeding high. As many have been astonished at thee, so shall his visage be inglorious among men," and St. Paul says, "He became obedient unto death, even to the death of the cross. For which cause God hath exalted him and hath given him a name which is above all names" (Phil. 2:8–9), that is to say, He shall be named God by all, and all shall pay Him reverence as God. And this is why St. Paul adds, "That in the name of Jesus every knee should bow, of those that are in heaven, on earth, and under the earth" (*ibid.* 10).

(iv) A power of judgment. For it is said, "Thy cause hath been judged as that of the wicked. Cause and judgment thou shalt recover" (Job 36:17).

(3.49.6.)

Fourth Tuesday

THE EXAMPLE OF CHRIST CRUCIFIED

Christ assumed human nature in order to restore fallen humanity. He had therefore to suffer and to do, according to human nature, the things which could serve as a remedy against the sin of the fall.

Man's sin consists in this that he so cleaves to bodily goods that he neglects what is good spiritually. It was therefore necessary for the Son of God to show this in the humanity he had taken, through all he did and suffered, so that men should repute temporal things, whether good or evil, as nothing, for otherwise, hindered by an exaggerated affection for them, they would be less devoted to spiritual things.

Christ therefore chose poor people for his parents, people nevertheless perfect in virtue, so that none of us should glory in the mere rank or wealth of our parents.

He led the life of a poor man, to teach us to set no store by wealth.

He lived the life of an ordinary man, without any rank, to wean men from an undue desire for honors.

Toil, thirst, hunger, the aches of the body—all these he endured, to encourage men, whom pleasures and delights attract, not to be deterred from virtue by the austerity a good life entails.

He went so far as to endure even death, lest the fear of death might at any time tempt man to abandon the truth. And lest any of us might dread to die even a shameful death for the truth, he chose to die by the most accursed death of all, by crucifixion.

That the Son of God, made man, should suffer death was also fitting for this reason, that by his example he stimulates our courage, and so makes true what St. Peter said, "Christ suffered for us, leaving you an example that you should follow his steps" (1 Pet. 2:21).   *(Contra Armen. Sarac. 7)*

Christ truly suffered for us, leaving us an example in anxieties, contempts, scourgings, the cross, death itself, that we might follow in his steps. If we endure for Christ our own anxieties and sufferings, we shall also reign together with Christ in the happiness that is everlasting. St. Bernard says: "How few are they, O Lord, who yearn to go after Thee, and yet there is no one that desireth not to come to Thee, for all men know that in Thy right hand are delights that will never fail. All desire to enjoy Thee, but not all to imitate Thee. They would willingly reign with Thee, but spare themselves from suffering with Thee. They have no desire to look for Thee, whom yet they desire to find."

(De humanitate Christi, cap. 47.)

Fourth Wednesday

The Divine Friend

His sisters sent to him saying: Lord, behold,
he whom thou lovest is sick.—John 11:3.

Three things here call for thought.

1. God's friends are from time to time afflicted in the body. It is not, therefore, in any way a proof that a man is not a friend of God that he is from time to time sick and ailing. Eliphaz argued falsely against Job when he said, "Remember, I pray thee, whoever perished being innocent? Or when were the just destroyed? (Job 4:7).

The gospel corrects this when it says, "Lord, behold, he whom thou lovest is sick," and the Book of Proverbs, too, where we read, "For whom the Lord loveth, be chastiseth: and as a father in the son he pleaseth himself (Prov. 3:12).

2. The sisters do not say, "Lord, come and heal him." They merely explain that Lazarus is ill; they say, "He is sick." This is to remind us that, when we are dealing with a friend, it is enough to

make known our necessity; we do not need to add a request. For a friend, since he wills the welfare of his friend as he wills his own, is as anxious to ward off evil from his friend as he is to ward it off from himself. This is true most of all in the case of Him who, of all friends, loves most truly. "The Lord keepeth all them that love him" (Ps. 144:20).

3. These two sisters, who so greatly desire the cure of their sick brother, do not come to Christ personally, as did the centurion and the man sick of the palsy. From the special love and familiarity which Christ had shown them, they had a special confidence in Him. And, possibly, their grief kept them at home, as St. Chrysostom thinks. "A friend if he continue steadfast, shall be to thee as thyself, and shall act with confidence among them of thy household" (Ecclus. 6:11).

(In John 11.)

Fourth Thursday

THE DEATH OF LAZARUS

1. "Lazarus our friend sleepeth" (John 11:11).

"Our friend"—for the many benefits and services he rendered us, and therefore we owe it not to fail in his necessity. "Sleepeth"—therefore we must come to his assistance: "a brother is proved in distress" (Prov. 17:17).

"He sleepeth," I say, as St. Augustine says, to the Lord. But to men he was dead, nor had they power to raise him.

"Sleep" is a word we use with various meanings. We use it to mean natural sleep, negligence, blameworthy inattention, the peace of contemplation, the peace of future glory, and we use it also to mean death. "We will not have you ignorant, concerning the last sleep, that you be not sorrowful, even as others that have no hope," says St. Paul (1 Thess. 4:12).

Death is called sleep because of the hope of resurrection, and so it has been customary to give death this name since the time when Christ died and was raised again: "I have slept and have taken my rest" (Ps. 3:6).

2. "I go that I may awake him out of sleep" (John 11:11).

In these words Jesus gives us to understand that he could raise Lazarus from the tomb as easily as we raise a sleeper from his bed. Nor is this to be wondered at, for He is none other than the Lord who "raiseth up the dead and giveth life" (John 5:21). And hence He is able to say, "The hour cometh when all that are in the graves shall hear the voice of the Son of God" (*ibid.* 5:28).

3. "Let us go to him" (John 11:15).

Here it is the mercifulness of God that we are shown. Men, living in sin and as it were dead, unable of any power of their own to come to him, He mercifully draws, anticipating their desire and need. Jeremiah speaks of this when he says, "Thus saith the Lord, I have loved thee with an everlasting love, therefore have I drawn thee, taking pity on thee" (Jer. 31:3).

4. "Jesus therefore came and found that he had been four days already in the grave" (John 11:17).

St. Augustine sees in the four-days dead Lazarus a figure of the fourfold spiritual death of the sinner. He dies intact through original sin, through actual sin against the natural law, through actual sin against the written law, through actual sin against the law of the gospel and of grace.

Another interpretation is that the first day represents the sin of the heart: "Take away the evil of your thoughts," says Isaiah (1:16); the second day represents sins of the tongue: "Let no evil speech proceed from your mouth," says St. Paul (Eph. 4:29); the third day represents the sins of evil action, "Cease to do perversely" (Isaiah 1:16); the fourth day stands for the sins of wicked habit.

Whatever explanation we give, Our Lord at times does heal those who are four days dead, that is, those who have broken the law of the gospel and are bound fast by habits of sin. *(In John 11.)*

Fourth Friday

THE PRECIOUS BLOOD

1. Through the blood of Christ the New Testament was confirmed. "This chalice is the new testament in my blood" (1 Cor. 11:25). Testament has a double meaning.

(i) It may mean any kind of agreement or pact.

Now God has twice made an agreement with mankind. In one pact God promised man temporal prosperity and deliverance from temporal losses, and this pact is called the Old Testament. In another pact God promised man spiritual blessings and deliverance from spiritual losses, and this is called the New Testament, "I will make a new covenant, saith the Lord, with the house of Israel and with the house of Juda: not according to the covenant which I made with their fathers, in the day that I took them by the hand to bring them out of the land of Egypt: but this shall be the covenant: I will give my law in their bosoms and I will write it in their hearts and I will be their God and they shall be my people" (Jer. 31:31–33).

Among the ancients it was customary to pour out the blood of some victim in confirmation of a pact. This Moses did when, taking the blood, he sprinkled it upon the people and he said, "This is the blood of the covenant which the Lord hath made with you" (Exod. 24:8). As the Old Testament or pact was thus confirmed in the figurative blood of oxen, so the New Testament or pact was confirmed in the blood of Christ, shed during his Passion.

(ii) Testament has another more restricted meaning when it signifies the arrangement of an inheritance among the different heirs, i.e., a will. Testaments, in this sense, are only confirmed by the death of the testator. As St. Paul says, "For a testament is of force, after men are dead: otherwise it is as yet of no strength, whilst the testator liveth" (Heb. 9:17). God, in the beginning, made an arrangement of the eternal inheritance we were to receive, but under the figure of temporal goods. This is the Old Testament. But afterward He made the New Testament, explicitly promising the eternal inheritance, which indeed was confirmed by the blood of the death of Christ. And therefore, Our Lord, speaking of this, says, "This chalice is the new testament in my blood" (1 Cor. 11:25), as though to say, "By that which is contained in this chalice, the new testament, confirmed in the blood of Christ, is commemorated."

(In 1 Cor. 12.)

2. There are other things which make the blood of Christ precious. It is:

(i) A cleansing of our sins and uncleanness. Jesus Christ hath "loved us and washed us from our sins in his own blood" (Apoc. 1:5).

(ii) Our redemption: "Thou hast redeemed us in Thy blood" (*ibid.* 5:9).

(iii) The peacemaker between us and God and his angels, "making peace through the blood of his cross, both as to the things that are on earth and the things that are in the heavens" (Coloss. 1:20).

(iv) A draught of life to all who receive it. "Drink ye all of this" (Matt. 26:27). "That they might drink the purest blood of the grape" (Deut. 32:14).

(v) The opening of the gate of heaven. "Having therefore, brethren, a confidence in the entering into the holies by the blood of Christ" (Heb. 10:19), that is to say, a continuous prayer for us to God. For His blood daily cries for us to the Father, as again we are told, "You are come to the sprinkling of blood which speaketh better than that of Abel" (*ibid.* 12:22–24). The blood of Abel called for punishment; the blood of Christ calls for pardon.

(vi) Deliverance of the saints from hell. "Thou also by the blood of thy testament hast sent forth thy prisoners out of the pit, wherein is no water" (Zech. 9:11).

(Sermon for Passion Sunday.)

Fourth Saturday

THERE WAS NOT ANY MORE FITTING WAY
TO FREE THE HUMAN RACE
THAN THROUGH THE PASSION OF CHRIST

The suitability of any particular way for the attainment of a given end is reckoned according to the greater or less number of things useful to that end which the way in question brings about. The more things helpful to the end the method chosen brings about, the better and more suitable is that method or way. Now owing to the fact that it was through the Passion of Christ that man was delivered, many things helpful to man's salvation came together in addition to his being freed from sin.

(i) Thanks to the fact that it was through the Passion that man was delivered, man learns how much God loves him, and is thereby stimulated to that love of God, in which is to be found the perfection of man's salvation. "God commendeth his charity towards us: because when as yet we were sinners, Christ died for us" (Rom. 5:8).

(ii) In the Passion He gave us an example of obedience, humility, constancy, justice, and of other virtues also, all of which we must practice if we are to be saved. "Christ suffered for us, leaving you an example that you should follow His steps" (1 Pet. 2:21).

(iii) Christ by His Passion not only delivered man from sin, but also merited for man the grace which makes him acceptable to God, and the glory of life with God for eternity.

(iv) The fact that it is through the Passion that man has been saved brings home to man the need of keeping himself clear from sin. Man has only to realize that it was at the price of the blood of Christ that he was bought back from sin. "You are bought with a great price. Glorify God and bear him in your body" (1 Cor. 6:20).

(v) The fact that the Passion was the way chosen heightens the dignity of human nature. As it was man that was deceived and conquered by the devil, so now it is man by whom the devil in turn is conquered. As it was man who once earned death, so it is man who, by dying, has overcome death. "Thanks be to God, who hath given us the victory through Our Lord Jesus Christ (1 Cor. 15:57).

(3.46.3.)

Passion Week—Sunday

THE PASSION OF CHRIST

As Moses lifted up the serpent in the desert, so must the Son of Man be lifted up: that whosoever believeth in him may not perish; but may have life everlasting.—John 3:14–15.

We may note here three things.

1. The Figure of the Passion. "As Moses lifted up the serpent in the desert." When the Jews said, "Our soul now loatheth this very light food" (Num. 21:5), the Lord sent serpents in punishment, and afterwards, for a remedy, He commanded the brazen serpent to be made as a remedy against the serpents and also as a figure of the Passion. It is the nature of a serpent to be poisonous, but the brazen serpent had no poison. It was but the figure of a poisonous serpent. So also Christ had no sin, which is the poison, but He had the likeness of sin. "God sent his own Son in the likeness of sinful flesh and of sin" (Rom. 8:3). Therefore Christ had the effect of the serpent against the movements of our blazing desires.

2. The Mode of the Passion. "So must the Son of Man be lifted up." This refers to His being raised upon the cross. He willed to die lifted up (i) To purify the air: already He had purified the earth by the holiness of His living there—it still remained for Him to purify, by His dying there, the air; (ii) To triumph over the devils,

who in the air, make their preparations to war on us; (iii) To draw our hearts to His heart: "I, if I be lifted up from the earth, will draw all things to myself" (John 12:32). Since in the death of the cross he was exalted, and since it was there that He overcame his enemies, we say that he was exalted rather than that he died. "He shall drink of the torrent by the way side; therefore shall He lift up His head (Ps. 109:7).

The cross was the cause of His exaltation. "He became obedient unto death, even to the death of the cross, wherefore God hath exalted Him" (Phil. 2:8).

3. The Fruit of the Passion. The fruit is eternal life. Whence Our Lord says Himself, "Whosoever believeth in Him, doing good works, may not perish, but may have life everlasting" (John 3:16).

And this fruit corresponds to the fruit of the serpent that foreshadowed Him. For whoever looked upon the brazen serpent was delivered from the poison and his life was preserved. Now the man who looks upon the Son of Man lifted up is the man who believes in Christ crucified, and it is in this way that he is delivered from the poison that is sin and preserved for the life that is eternal.

(In John 3.)

Passion Monday

THE PASSION OF CHRIST IS A REMEDY AGAINST SIN

We find in the Passion of Christ a remedy against all the evils that we incur through sin. Now these evils are five in number.

(i) We ourselves become unclean. When a man commits any sin he soils his soul, for just as virtue is the beauty of the soul, so sin is a stain upon it. "How happeneth it, O Israel, that thou art in thy enemies' land? Thou art grown old in a strange country, thou art defiled with the dead" (Baruch 3:10–11).

The Passion of Christ takes away this stain. For Christ, by His Passion, made of His blood a bath wherein He might wash sinners. The soul is washed with the blood of Christ in Baptism, for it is from the blood of Christ that the sacrament draws its power of giving new life. When therefore one who is baptized soils himself again by sin, he insults Christ and sins more deeply than before.

(ii) We offend God. As the man who is fleshly minded loves what is beautiful to the flesh, so God loves spiritual beauty, the beauty of the soul. When the soul's beauty is defiled by sin, God is offended and holds the offender in hatred. But the Passion of Christ takes away this hatred, for it does what man himself could not possibly do, namely, it makes full satisfaction to God for the sin. The love and obedience of Christ was greater than the sin and rebellion of Adam.

(iii) We ourselves are weakened. Man believes that, once he has committed the sin, he will be able to keep from sin for the future. Experience shows that what really happens is quite otherwise. The effect of the first sin is to weaken the sinner and make him still more inclined to sin. Sin dominates man more and more, and man left to himself, whatever his powers, places himself in such a state that he cannot rise from it. Like a man who has thrown himself into a well, there he must lie, unless he is drawn up by some divine power. After the sin of Adam, then, our human nature was weaker; it had lost its perfection, and men were more prone to sinning.

But Christ, although He did not utterly make an end of this weakness, nevertheless greatly lessened it. Man is so strengthened by the Passion of Christ—and the effect of Adam's sin is so weakened—that he is no longer dominated by it. Helped by the grace of God, given him in the sacraments, which derive their power from the Passion of Christ, man is now able to make an effort and so rise up from his sins. Before the Passion of Christ there were few who lived without mortal sin, but since the Passion many have lived and do live without it.

(iv) Liability to the punishment earned by sin. This the justice of God demanded, namely, that for each sin the sinner should be punished, the penalty to be measured according to the sin. Whence, since mortal sin is infinitely wicked, seeing that it is a sin against what is infinitely good, that is to say, God whose commands the sin despises, the punishment due to mortal sin is infinite too.

But by His Passion Christ took away from us this penalty, for He endured it Himself. "Who his own self bore our sins," that is, the punishment due to us for our sins, "in his body upon the tree" (1 Pet. 2:24).

So great was the power and value of the Passion of Christ that it was sufficient to expiate all the sins of all the world, reckoned by millions though they be. This is the reason why baptism frees the baptized from all their sins, and why the priest can forgive sin. This is why the man who more and more fashions his life in conformity with the Passion of Christ, and makes himself like to Christ in His Passion, attains an ever fuller pardon and ever greater graces.

(v) Banishment from the kingdom. Subjects who offend the king are sent into exile. So, too, man was expelled from Paradise. Adam, having sinned, was straightway thrown out and the gates barred against him.

But, by His Passion, Christ opened those gates and called back the exiles from banishment. As the side of Christ opened to the soldier's lance, the gates of heaven opened to man, and as Christ's blood flowed, the stain was washed out, God was appeased, our weakness taken away, amends made for our sins, and the exiles were recalled. Thus it was that Our Lord said immediately to the repentant thief, "This day thou shalt be with me in Paradise" (Luke 23:43). Such a thing was never before said to any man, not to Adam nor to Abraham, nor even to David. But "This day," the day on which the gate is opened, the thief does but ask and he finds. "Having confidence in the entering into the holies by the blood of Christ" (Heb. 10:19).   (In Symb.)

Passion Tuesday

THE BURIAL OF CHRIST

She hath wrought a good work upon me. She in pouring this ointment upon me hath done it for my burial. —Matt. 26:10-12.

It was right that Christ should be buried.

1. It proved that He had really died. No one is placed in the grave unless he is undeniably dead. And, as we read in St. Mark (ch. 15), Pilate, before he gave leave for Christ to be buried, made careful enquiry to assure himself that Christ was dead.

2. The very fact that Christ rose again from the grave gives a hope of rising again through Him to all others who lie in their graves. As it says in the gospel: "All that are in the grave shall hear the voice of the Son of God. And they that hear shall live" (John 5:28, 25).

3. It was an example for those who by the death of Christ are spiritually dead to sin, for those, that is, who are hidden away from the turmoil of human affairs. So St. Paul says, "You are dead; and your life is hid with Christ in God" (Col. 3:3). So, too, those who are baptized, since by the death of Christ they die to sin, are as it were buried with Christ in their immersion, as St. Paul again says, "We are buried together with Christ by baptism unto death" (Rom. 6:4).

As the death of Christ efficiently wrought our salvation, so too is his burial effective for us. St. Jerome, for example, says, "By the burial of Christ we all rise again," and explaining the words of Isaiah (53:9), "He shall give the ungodly for his burial," the Gloss says, "This means He shall give to God and the Father the nations lacking in filial devotion: for through his death and burial he has obtained possession of them."

The Psalm (Ps. 137:6) says, "I am become as a man without help, free among the dead." Christ by being buried showed himself free among the dead indeed, for His being enclosed in the tomb was not allowed to hinder His coming forth in the Resurrection.

(3.51.1.)

Passion Wednesday

On Being Buried Spiritually

The sepulcher is a figure by which is signified the contemplation of heavenly things. So, St. Gregory, commenting on the words of Job (3:22), "They rejoice exceedingly when they have found the grave," says: "As in the grave the body is hidden away when dead, so in divine contemplation there lies concealed the soul, dead to the world. There, at rest from the world's clamor, it lies in a three days' burial through, as it were, its triple immersion in baptism. 'Thou shalt hide them in the secret of thy face, from the disturbance of men' (Ps. 30:21). Those in great trouble, tormented with the hates of men, enter in spirit the presence of God and they are at rest."

Three things are required for this spiritual burial in God, namely, that the mind be perfected by the virtues; that the mind be all bright and shining with purity; and that it be wholly dead to this world. All these things are shown figuratively in the burial of Christ.

The first is shown in St. Mark's Gospel where we read how Mary Magdalen anointed Our Lord for His burial by anticipation, as it were. "She hath done what she could: she is come beforehand to anoint my body for the burial" (Mark 14:). The ointment of precious spikenard (ibid. 3) stands for the virtues, for it is a thing very precious, and in this life nothing is more precious than the virtues. The soul that wishes to be holy and to be buried in divine contemplation, must first, then, anoint itself by the exercise of the virtues. Job (5:26) says, "Thou shalt enter into the grave in abundance"—and the Gloss explains the grave as meaning here, "divine contemplation"—as a heap of wheat is brought in its season, and the explanation given in the Gloss is that eternal contemplation is the prize of a life of action, and therefore it must be that the perfect, first of all, exercise their souls in the virtues and then, afterward, bury them in the barn where all quiet is gathered.

The second of the three things required is also noted in St. Mark, where we read (15:46) that Joseph bought a winding sheet, that is, a sheet of fine linen, which is only brought to its dazzling whiteness with great labor. Hence it signifies that brightness of the soul, which also is not perfectly attained except with great labor. "He that is just, let him be justified still" (Apoc. 22:11). "Let us walk in newness of life" (Rom. 6:4), going from good to better, through the justice inaugurated by faith to the glory for which we hope. Therefore it is that men, bright with a spotless interior life, should be buried in the sepulcher of divine contemplation. St. Jerome, commenting on the words, "Blessed are the clean of heart, for they shall see God" (Matt. 5:8), says, "The clean Lord is seen by the clean of heart."

The third point for consideration is given by St. John where, in his gospel (19:30), he writes, "Nicodemus also came, bringing a mixture of myrrh and aloes, about an hundred pound weight." This hundred pounds weight of myrrh and aloes, brought to preserve the dead body, symbolizes that perfect mortification of the external senses, the means by which the spirit, dead to the world, is preserved from the vices that would corrupt it. "Though our outward wan is corrupted, yet the inward man is renewed day by day" (2 Cor. 4:16), which is as much as to say the inward man is most thoroughly purified from vices by the fire of tribulation.

Therefore man's soul must first, with Christ, become dead to this world, and then, afterward, be buried with him in the hiding place of divine contemplation. St. Paul says, "You are dead" with Christ, to the things that, are vain and fleeting, "and your life is hid with Christ in God" (Col. 3:3).

(De humanitate Christi, cap. 42.)

Passion Thursday

WHICH IS THE GREATEST SIGN OF HIS LOVE OUR LORD HAS GIVEN US?

It would seem that Christ gave us a greater sign of His love by giving us His body as our food than by suffering for us. For the love that will be in the life to come is a more perfect thing than the love that is in this life. And the benefit that Christ bestows on us by giving us His body as food is more like to the love of the life to come in which we shall fully enjoy God. The Passion that Christ underwent for us is, on the other hand, more like to the love that is of this life, in which we, too, are to suffer for Christ. Therefore it is a greater sign of Christ's love for us that he delivered His body to us as our food, than that He suffered for us.

Nevertheless, it is an argument against this that in St. John's gospel Our Lord himself says, "Greater love than this no man hath, that a man lay down his life for his friends" (John 15:13).

The strongest of human loves is the love with which a man loves himself. Therefore this love must be the measure, by comparison with which we estimate the love by which a man loves others than himself. Now the extent of a man's love for another is shown by the extent of good desired for himself that he forgoes for his friend. As Holy Scripture says, "He that neglecteth a loss for the sake of a friend, is just" (Prov. 12:26). Now a man wishes well to himself as to three things, namely, his soul, his body, and things outside himself.

It is then already a sign of love that, for another, a man is willing to suffer loss of things outside himself.

It is a greater sign if he is also willing to suffer loss in his body for another, that is, by bearing the burden of work or undergoing punishment.

It is the greatest of all signs of love if a man is willing, by dying for his friend, to lay down his very life.

Therefore, that Christ, in suffering for us, laid down His life was the greatest of all signs that He loved us. That He has given us His body for our food in the sacrament does not entail for Him any loss. It follows then that the first is the greater sign. Also this sacrament is a kind of memorial and figure of the Passion of Christ. But the truth is always greater than that which figures it, the thing is always greater than the memorial that recalls it.

The showing forth of the body of Christ in the sacrament has about it, it is true, a certain figure of the love with which God loves us in the life to come. But Christ's Passion is associated with that love itself, by which God calls us from perdition to the life to come. The love of God, however, is not greater in the life to come than it is in this present life. *(Quodlibeta 5 q 3 a 2.)*

Passion Friday

Our Lady's Suffering in the Passion

Thy own soul a sword shall pierce.—Luke 2:35.

In these words there is noted for us the close association of Our Lady with the Passion of Christ. Four things especially made the Passion most bitter for her.

Firstly, the goodness of her son, "Who did no sin" (1 Pet. 2:22).

Secondly, the cruelty of those who crucified Him, shown, for example, in this that as He lay dying they refused Him even water, nor would they allow His mother, who would most lovingly have given it, to help Him.

Thirdly, the disgrace of the punishment: "Let us condemn him to a most shameful death" (Wis. 2:20).

Fourthly, the cruelty of the torment. "O ye that pass by the way, attend and see if there be any sorrow like to my sorrow" (Lam. 1:12). *(Serm.)*

The words of Simeon, "Thy own soul a sword shall pierce," Origen, and other doctors with him, explain with reference to the pain felt by Our Lady in the Passion of Christ. St. Ambrose, however, says that by the sword is signified Our Lady's prudence, thanks to which she was not without knowledge of the heavenly mystery. For the word of God is a living thing, strong and keener than the keenest sword (cf. Heb. 4:12).

Other writers again, St. Augustine for example, understand by the sword the stupefaction that overcame Our Lady at the death of her Son, not the doubt that goes with lack of faith but a certain fluctuation of bewilderment, a staggering of the mind. St. Basil, too, says that as Our Lady stood by the cross with all the detail of the Passion before her, and in her mind the testimony of Gabriel, the message that words cannot tell of her divine conception, and all the vast array of miracles, her mind swayed, for she saw Him the victim of such vileness, and yet knew Him for the author of such wonders.

(3.27.4 ad 2.)

Although Our Lady knew by faith that it was God's will that Christ should suffer, and although she brought her will into unity with God's will in this matter, as the saints do, nevertheless, sadness filled her soul at the death of Christ. This was because her lower will revolted at the particular thing she had willed, and this is not contrary to perfection.

(1 Dist. 48 q unica a 3.)

Passion Saturday

How We, Each of Us, Should Wash One Another's Feet

*If I then being your Lord and Master,
have washed your feet; you also ought
to wash one another's feet.*—John 13:14.

Our Lord wishes that His disciples shall imitate His example. He says therefore, "If I," who am the greater, being your master and the Lord, "have washed your feet, you also," all the more who are the less, who are disciples, slaves even, "ought to wash one another's feet." "Whosoever will be the greater among you, let him be your minister. . . . Even as the Son of Man is not come to be ministered unto, but to minister" (Matt. 20:26–28).

St. Augustine says every man ought to wash the feet of his fellows, either actually or in spirit. And it is by far the best, and true beyond all controversy, that we should do it actually, lest Christians scorn to do what Christ did. For when a man bends his body to the feet of a brother, human feeling is stirred up in his very heart, or, if it be there already, it is strengthened. If we cannot actually wash his feet, at least we can do it in spirit. The washing of the feet signifies the washing away of stains. You therefore wash the feet of your brother when, as far as lies in your power, you wash away his stains. And this you may do in three ways:

(i) By forgiving the offenses he has done to you. "Forgiving one another, if any have a complaint against another: even as the Lord hath forgiven you, so do you also" (Coloss. 3:13).

(ii) By praying for the forgiveness of his sin, as St. James bids us, "Pray for one another, that you may be saved" (James 5:16). This way of washing, like the first, is open to all the faithful.

(iii) The third way is for prelates, who should wash by forgiving sins through the authority of the keys, according to the gospel,

"Receive ye the Holy Ghost; whose sins you shall forgive, they are forgiven them (John 20:23).

We can also say that in this one act Our Lord showed all the works of mercy. He who gives bread to the hungry, washes his feet, as also does the man who harbors the harborless or he who clothes the naked.

"Communicating to the necessities of the saints" (Rom. 12:13).   (*In John 13.*)

Holy Week—Palm Sunday

CHRIST'S PASSION SERVES US AS AN EXAMPLE

The Passion of Christ is by itself sufficient to form us in every virtue. For whoever wishes to live perfectly need do no more than scorn what Christ scorned on the cross, and desire what He there desired. There is no virtue of which, from the cross, Christ does not give us an example.

If you seek an example of charity, "Greater love than this no man hath, than that a man lay down His life for his friends" (John 15:13), and this Christ did on the cross. And since it was for us that He gave his life, it should not be burdensome to bear for Him whatever evils come our way. "What shall I render to the Lord, for all the things that He hath rendered to me" (Ps. 115:12).

If you seek an example of patience, in the cross you find the best of all. Great patience shows itself in two ways. Either when a man suffers great evils patiently, or when he suffers what he could avoid and forbears to avoid. Now Christ on the cross suffered great evils. "O all ye that pass by the way, attend and see, if there be any sorrow like to my sorrow" (Lam. 1:12). "And He suffered them patiently, for, when he suffered he threatened not" (1 Pet. 2:23) but led as a sheep to the slaughter, he was "dumb as a lamb before his shearer" (Isaiah 53:7).

Also it was in His power to avoid the suffering and He did not avoid it. "Thinkest thou that I cannot ask my Father, and he will give me presently more than twelve legions of angels?" (Matt. 26:53). The patience of Christ, then, on the cross was the greatest patience ever shown. "Let us run by patience to the fight proposed to us: looking on Jesus, the author and finisher of faith, who having joy set before Him, endured the cross, despising the shame" (Heb. 12:1-2).

If you seek an example of humility, look at the crucified. For it is God who wills to be judged and to die at the will of Pontius Pilate. "Thy cause hath been judged as that of the wicked" (Job 36:17). Truly as that of the wicked, for "Let us condemn him to a most shameful death" (Wis. 2:20). The Lord willed to die for the slave, the life of the angels for man.

If you seek an example of obedience, follow Him who "became obedient unto death" (Phil. 2:8), "for as by the disobedience of one man, many were made sinners; so also by the obedience of one, many shall be made just" (Rom. 5:19).

If you seek an example in the scorning of the things of this world, follow Him who is the King of Kings, and the Lord of Lords, in whom are all the treasures of wisdom. Lo! On the cross He hangs naked, fooled, spit upon, beaten, crowned with thorns, sated with gall and vinegar, and dead. "My garments they parted among them; and upon my vesture they cast lots" (Ps. 21:19).

Error to crave for honors, for He was exposed to blows and to mockery. Error to seek titles and decorations, for "platting a crown of thorns, they put it upon His head, and a reed in his right hand. And bowing the knee before him, they mocked him, saying Hail, king of the Jews" (Matt. 27:29).

Error to cling to pleasures and comfort, for "they gave me gall for my food, and in my thirst they gave me vinegar to drink" (Ps. 68:22).

(In Symb.)

Monday in Holy Week

IT IS NECESSARY THAT WE BE WHOLLY CLEAN

1. "If I wash thee not, thou shalt have no part with me" (John 13:8). No one can be made a sharer in the inheritance of eternity, a co-heir with Christ, unless he is spiritually cleansed, for in the Apocalypse it is so stated. "There shall not enter info it anything defiled" (Apoc. 21:27), and in the Psalms we read, "Lord who shall dwell in thy tabernacle?" (Ps. 14:1). "Who shall ascend into the mountain of the Lord; or who shall stand in his holy place? The innocent in hands, and clean of heart" (Ps. 23:3–4).

It is therefore as though Our Lord said, "If I wash thee not," thou shalt not be cleansed, and if thou art not cleansed, "thou shalt have no part with me."

2. "Simon Peter saith to him: Lord, not only my feet but also my hands and my head" (John 13:9).

Peter, utterly stricken, offers his whole self to be washed, so confounded is he with love and with fear. We read, in fact, in the book called *The Journeying of Clement*, that Peter used to be so over come by the bodily presence of Our Lord, which he had most fervently loved, that whenever, after Our Lord's Ascension, the memory of that dearest presence and most holy company came to him, he used so to melt into tears, that his cheeks seemed all worn out with them.

We can consider three parts in man's body: the head, which is the highest; the feet, which are the lowest part; and the hands which lie in between. In the interior man, that is to say, in the soul, there are likewise three parts. Corresponding to the head there is the higher reason, the power by means of which the soul clings to God. For the hands there is the lower reason by which the soul operates in good works. For the feet there are the senses and the feelings and desires arising from them. Now Our Lord knew the disciples to be clean as far as the head was concerned, for He knew they were joined to God by faith and by charity. He knew their hands also were clean, for He knew their good works. But as to their feet, He knew that the disciples were still somewhat entangled in those inclinations to earthly things that derive out of the life of the senses.

Peter, alarmed by Our Lord's warning (verse 8), not only consented that his feet should be washed, but begged that his hands and his head should be washed, too.

"Lord," he said, "not only my feet, but also my hands and my head." As though to say: "I know not whether hands and head need to be washed. 'For I am not conscious to myself of anything,' yet am I not 'hereby justified' (1 Cor. 4:4). Therefore I am ready not only for my feet to be washed, that is, those inclinations that arise out of the life of my senses, but also my hands, that is, my works, and my head, too, that is, my higher reason."

3. "Jesus saith to him: He that is washed needeth not but to wash his feet, but is clean wholly. And you are clean" (John 13:10). Origen, commenting on this text, says that the Apostles were clean, but needed to be yet cleaner. For reason should ever desire gifts that are better still, should ever set itself to achieve the very heights of virtue, should aspire to shine with the brightness of justice itself. "He that is holy, let him be sanctified still" (Apoc. 22:11).

(In John 13.)

Tuesday in Holy Week

CHRIST PREPARING TO WASH THE APOSTLE'S FEET

*He riseth from supper, and layeth aside his garments,
and having taken a towel, girded himself.*—John 13:4.

i. Christ, in his lowly office, shows Himself truly to be a servant, in keeping with His own words, "The Son of Man is not come to be ministered, but to minister, and to give His life a redemption for many" (Matt. 20:28).

Three things are looked for in a good servant or minister:

(i) That he should be careful to keep before him the numerous details in which his serving may so easily fall short. Now for a servant to sit or to lie down during his service is to make this necessary supervision impossible. Hence it is that servants stand. And therefore the gospel says of Our Lord, "He riseth from supper." Our Lord himself also asks us, "For which is greater, he that sitteth at table or he that serveth?" (Luke 22:27).

(ii) That he should show dexterity in doing at the right time all the things his particular office calls for. Now elaborate dress is a hindrance to this. Therefore Our Lord layeth aside his garments. And this was foreshadowed in the Old Testament when Abraham chose servants who were well appointed (Gen. 14:14).

(iii) That he should be prompt, having ready to hand all the things he needs. St. Luke (10:40) says of Martha that "she was busy about much serving." This is why Our Lord, having taken a towel, girded himself. Thus he was ready not only to wash the feet, but also to dry them. So He (who "came from God and goeth to God"—John 13:3), as He washes their feet, crushes down forever our swollen, human self-importance.

2. "After that, he putteth water into a basin, and began to wash" (John 13:5). We are given for our consideration this service of Christ; and in three ways his humility is set for our example.

(i) The kind of service this was, for it was the lowest kind of service of all! The Lord of all majesty bending to wash the feet of his slaves.

(ii) The number of services it contained, for, we are told, he put water into a basin, he washed their feet, he dried them, and so forth.

(iii) The method of doing the service, for He did not do it through others, nor even with others helping him. He did the service Himself. "The greater thou art, the more humble thyself in all things" (Ecclus. 3:20).

(In John 13.)

Holy Wednesday

THREE THINGS ARE SYMBOLIZED
BY THE WASHING OF THE FEET

He putteth water into a basin, and began to wash
the feet of the disciples, and to wipe them with the towel
wherewith he was girded.—John 13:5.

There are three things which this can be taken to symbolize.

1. The pouring of the water into the basin is a symbol of the pouring out of His blood upon the earth. Since the blood of Jesus has a power of cleansing, it may in a sense be called water. The reason why water, as well as blood, came out of His side, was to show that this blood could wash away sin.

Again we might take the water as a figure of Christ's Passion. "He putteth water into a basin," that is, by faith and devotion He stamped into the minds of faithful followers the memory of His Passion. "Remember my poverty, and transgression, the wormwood and the gall" (Lam. 3:19).

2. By the words "and began to wash" it is human imperfection

that is symbolized. For the Apostles, after their living with Christ, were certainly more perfect, and yet they needed to be washed, there were still stains upon them. We are here made to understand that no matter what is the degree of any man's perfection, he still needs to be made more perfect still; He is still contracting uncleanness of some kind to some extent. So in the Book of Proverbs we read, "Who can say My heart is clean, I am pure from sin" (Prov. 20:9).

Nevertheless the Apostles and the just have this kind of uncleanness only in their feet.

There are however others who are infected, not only in their feet, but wholly and entirely. Those who make their bed upon the soiling attractions of the world are made wholly unclean thereby. Those who wholly, that is to say, with their senses and with their wills, cleave to their desire of earthly things, these are wholly unclean.

But they who do not thus lie down, they who stand, that is, they who, in mind and in desire, are tending towards heavenly things, contract this uncleanness in their feet. Whoever stands must, necessarily, touch the earth at least with his feet. And we, too, in this life, where we must, to maintain life, make use of earthly things, cannot but contract a certain uncleanness, at least as far as those desires and inclinations are concerned which begin in our senses.

Therefore Our Lord commanded His disciples to shake off the dust from their feet. The text says, "He began to wash," because this washing away on earth of the affection for earthly things is only a beginning. It is only in the life to come that it will be really complete.

Thus by putting water into the basin, the pouring out of His blood is signified, and by His beginning to wash the feet of His disciples the washing away of our sins.

3. There is symbolized finally Our Lord's taking upon Him the punishment due to our sins. Not only did He wash away our sins but He also took upon Himself the punishment that they had earned. For our pains and our penances would not suffice were they not founded in the merit and the power of the Passion of Christ.

And this is shown in His wiping the feet of the disciples with the linen towel, that is the towel which is His body.

(In John 13.)

Maundy Thursday

THE LAST SUPPER

It was most fitting that the sacrament of the body of the Lord should have been instituted at the Last Supper.

1. Because of what that sacrament contains. For that which is contained in it is Christ Himself. When Christ in His natural appearance was about to depart from His disciples, He left Himself to them in a sacramental appearance, just as in the absence of the emperor there is exhibited the emperor's image. Whence St. Eusebius says: "Since the body he had assumed was about to be taken away from their bodily sight, and was about to be carried to the stars, it was necessary that, on the day of His last supper, He should consecrate for us the sacrament of His body and blood, so that what, as a price, was offered once should, through a mystery, be worshiped unceasingly."

2. Because without faith in the Passion there can never be salvation. Therefore it is necessary that there should be, forever, among men something that would represent the Lord's Passion, and the chief of such representative things in the Old Testament was the Paschal Lamb. To this there succeeded in the New Testament the sacrament of the Eucharist, which is commemorative of the past Passion of the Lord as the Paschal Lamb was a foreshadowing of the Passion to come.[5]

---

5. *Quod est rememorativum praeteritae Dominicae Passionis, sicut et illud fuit futurae praefigurativum.*

And therefore was it most fitting that, on the very eve of the Passion, the old sacrament of the Paschal Lamb having been celebrated, Our Lord should institute the new sacrament.

3. Because the last words of departing friends remain longest in the memory, our love being at such moments most tenderly alert. Nothing can be greater in the realm of sacrifice than that of the body and blood of Christ; no offering can be more effective. And hence, in order that the sacrament might be held in all the more veneration, it was in His last leave-taking of the Apostles that Our Lord instituted it.

Hence St. Augustine says, "Our savior, to bring before our minds with all His power the heights and the depths of this sacrament, willed, ere He left the disciples to go forth to His Passion, to fix it in their hearts and their memories as His last act."

Let us note that this sacrament has a threefold meaning:

(i) In regard to the past, it is commemorative of the Lord's Passion, which was a true sacrifice, and because of this the sacrament is called a sacrifice.

(ii) In regard to a fact of our own time, that is, to the unity of the church and that through this sacrament mankind should be gathered together. Because of this the sacrament is called communion.

St. John Damascene says the sacrament is called communion because by means of it we communicate with Christ, and this because we hereby share in His body and in His divinity, and because by it we are communicated to and united with one another.

(iii) In regard to the future, the sacrament foreshadows that enjoyment of God which shall be ours in our fatherland. On this account the sacrament is called *viaticum*, since it provides us with the means of journeying to that fatherland.

And on this account, too, the sacrament is also called Eucharist, that is to say, the good grace, either because the grace of God is life eternal, or because it really contains Christ who is the fullness of grace. In Greek the sacrament is also called *Metalipsis*, that is, Assumption, for through the sacrament we assume the divinity of the Son of God.

(De Humanitate Christi.)

Good Friday

THE DEATH OF CHRIST

That Christ should die was expedient.

1. To make our redemption complete. For, although any suffering of Christ had an infinite value, because of its union with His divinity, it was not by no matter which of His sufferings that the redemption of mankind was made complete, but only by His death. So the Holy Spirit declared speaking through the mouth of Caiaphas, "It is expedient for you that one man shall die for the people" (John 11:50). Whence St. Augustine says, "Let us stand in wonder, rejoice, be glad, love, praise, and adore, since it is by the death of our Redeemer that we have been called from death to life, from exile to our own land, from mourning to joy."

2. To increase our faith, our hope and our charity. With regard to faith the Psalm says (Ps. 140:10), "I am alone until I pass" from this world, that is, to the Father. When I shall have passed to the Father, then shall I be multiplied. "Unless the grain of wheat falling into the ground die, itself remaineth alone" (John 12:24).

As to the increase of hope, St. Paul writes, "He that spared not even his own Son, but delivered him up for us all, how hath he not also, with him, given us all things?" (Rom. 8:32). God cannot deny us this, for to give us all things is less than to give His own Son to death for us. St. Bernard says, "Who is not carried away to hope and confidence in prayer, when he looks on the crucifix and sees how Our Lord hangs there, the head bent as though to kiss, the arms outstretched in an embrace, the hands pierced to give, the side opened to love, the feet nailed to remain with us."

"Come, my dove, in the clefts of the rock" (Cant. 2:14). It is in the wounds of Christ the Church builds its nest and waits, for it is in the Passion of Our Lord that she places her hope of salvation, and thereby trusts to be protected from the craft of the falcon, that is, of the devil.

With regard to the increase of charity, Holy Scripture says, "At noon he burneth the earth" (Ecclus. 43:3), that is to say, in the fervor of His Passion He burns up all mankind with His love. So St. Bernard says, "The chalice thou didst drink, O good Jesus, maketh thee lovable above all things." The work of our redemption easily, brushing aside all hindrances, calls out in return the whole of our love. This it is which more gently draws out our devotion, builds it up more straightly, guards it more closely, and fires it with greater ardor.

3. Because our salvation is wrought in the manner of a sacrament, we dying to this world in a likeness to His death, "So that my soul chooseth hanging, and my bones death" (Job 7:15). St. Gregory says: "The soul is the mind's aspiration; the bones are the strength of the body's desires. Things hanged are raised thereby from the depths. The soul, then, is hanged to things eternal that the bones may die, for it is with the love of eternal life that the soul slays the strong attraction earthly things possess for it."

It is a sign that a soul is dead to the world when a soul is despised by the world. Again, to quote St. Gregory, "The sea keeps the bodies that are alive in it. Once they are dead it quickly casts them up."

(De Humanitate Christi, cap. 47.)

Holy Saturday

WHY OUR LORD WENT DOWN TO LIMBO

From the descent of Christ to hell we may learn, for our instruction, four things:

1. Firm hope in God. No matter what the trouble in which a man finds himself, he should always put trust in God's help and rely on it. There is no trouble greater than to find oneself in hell. If then Christ freed those who were in hell, any man who is a friend of God cannot but have great confidence that he too shall be freed from whatever anxiety holds him. "Wisdom forsook not the just when he was sold, but delivered him from sinners; she went down with him into the pit and in bands she left him not" (Wis. 10:13–14). And since to His servants God gives a special assistance, he who serves God should have still greater confidence. "He that feareth the Lord shall tremble at nothing, and shall not be afraid: for he is his hope" (Ecclus. 34:16).

2. We ought to conceive fear and to rid our selves of presumption. For although Christ suffered for sinners, and went down into hell to set them free, he did not set all sinners free, but only those who were free of mortal sin. Those who had died in mortal sin He left there. Wherefore for those who have gone down to hell in mortal sin there remains no hope of pardon. They shall be in hell as the holy Fathers are in heaven, that is forever.

3. We ought to be full of care. Christ went down into hell for our salvation, and we should be careful frequently to go down there too, turning over in our minds hell's pain and penalties, as did the holy king Hezekiah as we read in the prophecy of Isaiah, "I said: In the midst of my days I shall go to the gates of hell" (Isaiah 38:10).

Those who in their meditation often go down to hell during life, will not easily go down there at death. Such meditations are a powerful arm against sin, and a useful aid to bring a man back from sin. Daily we see men kept from evildoing by the fear of the law's punishments. How much greater care should they not take on account of the punishment of hell, greater in its duration, in its bitterness and in its variety. "Remember thy last end and thou shalt never sin" (Ecclus. 7:40).

4. The fact is for us an example of love. Christ went down into hell to set free those that were his own. We, too, therefore, should go down there to help our own. For those who are in purgatory are themselves unable to do anything, and therefore we ought to help them. Truly he would be a harsh man indeed who failed to come to the aid of a kinsman who lay in prison, here on earth. How much more harsh, then, the man who will not aid the friend who is in purgatory, for there is no comparison between the pains there and the pains of this world. "Have pity on me, have pity on me, at least you my friends, because the hand of the Lord hath touched me" (Job 19:21).

We help the souls in purgatory chiefly by these three means: by masses, by prayers, and by almsgiving. Nor is it wonderful that we can do so, for even in this world a friend can make satisfaction for a friend.

(In Symb.)

Made in the USA
Coppell, TX
24 February 2020